THE TRURO MURDERS

THE SEX KILLING SPREE THROUGH THE EYES OF AN ACCOMPLICE

RYAN GREEN

Disclaimer

This book is about real people committing real crimes. The story has been constructed by facts but some of the scenes, dialogue and characters have been fictionalised.

Polite Note to the Reader

This book is written in British English except where fidelity to other languages or accents are appropriate. Some words and phrases may differ from US English.

For Helen, Harvey, Frankie and Dougie

CONTENTS

Introduction

James Miller would have considered himself to be an accomplished liar if he had known what the word accomplished meant. In the moment when he was telling a lie to someone's face he could see in their eyes that they believed every word. If he got caught out after the fact by people going away and getting different answers, that was hardly his fault. His lying was top notch. It was just his planning ahead that caused him problems. He wasn't sure why people wanted to believe him so badly. Maybe it was because the thought of someone who looked and acted like him outsmarting them was too embarrassing. Maybe it was because, despite his failings, James was completely earnest in everything that he said to people, whether the things he was saying were true or not. Maybe people just couldn't believe that he was smart enough to remember a lie for as long as their conversation ran.

Even tonight his lying had been going perfectly right up until the moment he got out of the car, but now that he was sitting here in the dark with his back resting against a tree and the yellow moon was scowling down at him like the eye of God, he found that the bottomless well of deception was running dry just when he needed it the most. When he needed to convince himself that everything was going to turn out all right.

He had lied to that girl in the car. There were no two ways about it. He had told her things that were not true because that is what Chris would have wanted. When he offered to give her a ride, she had trusted him. He hadn't even had to lie then. She thought that she was safe with him just because of who he was, because of what he was, and he had let her go on believing it. It wasn't even a lie. He was exactly what he looked like. He was as harmless as he seemed. Even now she probably thought that she would have a little bit of fun with the hottest guy she had ever seen and then his funny queer friend was going to drive her home safe and sound. It was unbelievable. Even as James was telling himself that soon he would go back to the car and find her and Chris cuddled up happily on the back seat, he found that he couldn't swallow the lie.

This time James had chosen not to learn her name. She probably introduced herself just like a normal person, but he had been careful not to listen too closely. Just like he was trying not to listen too closely to what was happening in the car right now. He knew that there were sounds coming out of the car but he was the only person around for miles who might hear them. He had told himself that it might be easier if he didn't know her name. As if a name was all that made a person into a person. Lying to himself had always come just as easily to James as lying to other people. Growing up in rural Australia with a taste for other men meant that you had to lie every moment of the day just to survive. Any little slip, any lisp or limp wrist might mean that the men you met in the alley outside a bar were there for a very different sort of entertainment than you might have hoped. It hurt a little to hide every part of himself from the world outside, but it made it all the more special to share himself with someone like Chris. He had been practising lying to himself for decades. From little lies like "not knowing her name will make it easier" up through "maybe everything will be all right tonight" and all the way up to the big crazy ones like "maybe Chris will realise that he loves me and stop all this."

Deep in his squirming gut, James knew that every one of those things was a lie. He squeezed his eyes shut against the moonlight and pressed his back into the tree, feeling the bark bite into him through his sweat-soaked shirt. He pretended that it was Chris. That the comforting steady weight on his back was the man he loved. That Chris was here with him. Not over there with her. He was able to convince himself for all of a second before reality intruded. The sound was muffled by the car, by the distance and by the thickness of the humid night air. It was a woman's scream, cut off short. Straight-up denial wasn't going to work tonight, but there were a whole load of grey areas that James could still lurk in. Maybe tonight wasn't going to be a good night, where the girl went away with a smile on her face, but she might still walk away. Chris might have had to get a little rough with her to get what he wanted and that was okay. That was fine. James didn't like the long tense silence in the car as they drove a girl back after she had said no to Chris at the wrong time, but he could live with it. He could even convince himself that it was their fault sometimes. They might cry their crocodile tears but they knew why they were getting in the car. They knew how hot Chris was and what he wanted. Why did they have to play hard to get? These girls had no sense, coming out here to the middle of nowhere with two strange men. It didn't matter that Chris was gorgeous and charming or that James was funny and soothed all of their worries. They still made their own decisions, and they needed to live with the consequences.

That lie crumbled to ashes just the same as the rest of them. James knew what he was going to find when he walked back to the car. He knew it with dead certainty. There would have been rope no matter what happened in that car tonight. Chris wouldn't take a girl without a rope. That was his kink, tying people up. Nobody could complain about that—it didn't hurt anybody. Most of the girls liked it. It made them feel naughty or something. Sometimes James stayed in the car while Chris tied them up, as some extra reassurance for the girl, but it always felt a little too much like participating. You could feel the heat rolling off Chris, that electric energy that clung to him when he was excited. Sometimes Chris liked to practice his knots on James, and those were good nights and sweet memories that would keep him warm through the years to come, but they were just similar enough to what was happening in that car to raise bile up into James' mouth when he tried to call them up now.

He couldn't keep doing this. Chris might have had the stomach for it, but James couldn't do this anymore. It used to just be once in a while that they would go out cruising for a girl, but now it seemed to be every other night. Chris needed it again sooner and sooner each time and now it felt like he wasn't satisfied even when they did have a good night. On the nights when Chris found a girl and she went home happy, he was still angry and buzzing. Whatever he got out of his encounters with those girls was dwindling. He had to keep pushing further every time. To start with he just picked them up. Then he started to tie them up, too. Then he started to force them when they tried to say no, but now it was like even that was boring him. Like he needed to go one step further or the night hadn't been worthwhile. There were other sounds coming from the car, torturous sounds for James. The sound of Chris getting closer and closer and silence from the girl. He knew those sounds so intimately, better than he knew the sound of his own voice. They were seared into his memory. Every rumble from deep inside Chris' chest and every gasp that escaped his lips.

James sprung up from his spot in the dirt and walked away from the car as fast as his legs would carry him. He didn't need to listen to this. He might have gotten some prurient pleasure out of it before, but not anymore. Not knowing what was coming next. Or knowing what was probably already happening. He hiked away into the dark and tried not to keep count in his head. He had been counting the minutes since he left the car just the same as usual, but this time he wasn't coming back. He would just walk on into the dark until he came out the other side. On the other side of this night, there was no more longing and no more blood. If he just kept on walking he would never have to go back, never have to deal with all of the chaos and the madness that Chris left in his wake. He would never get to see Chris again. His stride faltered and he ground to a halt. He knew that he was just being crazy, thinking that he could walk away from all this. The only way that he was ever getting out was when Chris got bored of him and discarded him at the side of the road or dumped him in the wilderness like all of his other girls. James shivered. That thought shouldn't have made him happy. The thought that he might end up spent and used and tossed aside like trash should not have been his greatest ambition, but at least it would mean that Chris was looking at him again.

Looking at him with that fire in his eyes. Looking at him like he cared, at least for that moment. As if Chris loved him back for that one glorious moment as the ropes bit into his skin and the fingers tightened around his throat.

He stopped and stared out over the rolling green land, turned grey and unhealthy by the dim light. How had he come to this? How had he gone from being a person with hopes and dreams to being nothing more than a prop for Chris? James could see him in his mind right then, not the thing that he became in that car in the dark of night, but the real Chris who he had met so long ago. The Chris who was there for him when prison got too much. The Chris who had slapped him on the back when they both stepped outside together as free men for the first time, who took him for a beer and helped him to find a job. That Chris was still in there, that Chris was still back in the car, and in the end, Chris was worth it. He was worth the screaming and the sobbing and scrubbing stains off the car's upholstery. He was worth the dragging and the digging and the wild-eyed stares. Chris was worth going back to jail for, so why was James standing out here alone in the dark when the count in his head was telling him that long enough had passed, that the girl and Chris would both be done one way or the other?

He drew in a deep breath of the night air and then walked back to the steamed-up car with a new resolve settling his stomach. He would do what he had to do for Chris, just the same as he always had done. Besides, maybe tonight would be a good night and the girl would still be breathing by the time that he got there. It wasn't a lie to say maybe.

Chris was leaning on the bonnet of the car smoking when James arrived, looking like some black-and-white movie star and, despite it all, when he met his gaze James couldn't help but smile.

A Jailbird in Love

James William Miller did not have the best start in life. He was born on the second of February 1940 into a family that was already struggling. There were five other children in the family, five other mouths that needed to be fed and five other sets of needs that had to be addressed before quiet James was even noticed. The effect of the neglect was almost immediate. As soon as he was able to walk, he started trying to walk away. He ran away from home repeatedly as a young child, and was returned to his parents just as often by the local police who quickly came to see the boy as a troublemaker and nuisance rather than recognising the behaviour as a cry for help. The late 40s and early 50s were a very different time in Australia, when things that we would now consider to be child abuse were commonplace as "discipline." In later life, James refused to speak about his childhood, so it remains unclear what happened in that cramped family home to make a boy as young as four try to flee from his parents' care, but by the time that he was eleven, he finally had a permanent means of escape.

In light of his family issues and constant absences, it should come as no surprise that James struggled in school. Combined with the "disciplinary problems" that the boy faced, it wasn't long before the local teachers were looking for an alternate solution to having him disrupt their classes and grading curve. He was shipped off to Magill Reformatory School for Protestant Boys. The reformatory was not the relief that James might have hoped for. The building itself was a towering three-story-tall stone house in the Victorian style. It looked more like a prison than a boarding school and fulfilled a very similar function: segregating those children who society had deemed beyond saving from the general population. The only lessons that were given to the boys that were confined there were in obedience, and like all the others, James took to those teachings very poorly.

The only slight glimmer of a silver lining to this terrible time in James' life is that in the reformatory, while he was locked in close quarters with all the other boys his age who "acted inappropriately," he came to discover the truth about his sexuality as it was emerging. He didn't form any lasting relationships with the boys from the reformatory, but he made his first fumbling steps towards the possibility of a healthy relationship in his future. Even if the constant fear of rejection made him flinch away from anything like a serious commitment, the possibility of emotional fulfilment presented itself for the first time in his life.

James left the reformatory as soon as he was able with no formal education and no prospects for the future. With no home and few hopes for the future, he made a little money travelling around Australia and working as an itinerant labourer. He would receive less pay than the workers who were on the books of the work gangs, but because he was paid under the table he didn't have to pay tax, so he managed to convince himself that it balanced out. Before long he hit a dry spell. Labouring work is notoriously seasonal, so when winter came on he was left with no source of income and nowhere to shelter from the cold. James made the only decision that would let him survive. He began to steal.

In the beginning, his crimes were minor ones, born mostly from opportunity, but gradually taking the risk of stealing a loaf of bread so that he could eat for a day developed into the far less frequent risk of stealing a car, which he could sell along to eat for a month. He had no particular talent for crime, and over the course of his 20 years he was convicted 30 times for car theft, larceny, breaking and entering, purse-snatching, and stealing. None of his crimes were ever violent. In fact, he seemed to have a personal aversion to violence that seems incongruous to his life of crime. But what he lacked in violence and talent he made up for in persistence. Every time that he was released from prison, he immediately made contact with the few criminals foolish enough to go on fencing his stolen goods and returned to his pursuit of enough wealth to support his meagre needs. He would often seek out legal work, but his prospects did not improve as he grew older. While he was relatively pleasant, he was clearly uneducated, clearly homosexual, and incapable of masking either of these traits when confronted with something as daunting as a job interview. He did brief stints in factories, worked for a little longer in labouring jobs, but every time he was drawn back into the criminal underworld due to the absolute lack of care that anyone in the "real world" felt towards him and all of the thousands of others like him. At age 34, he returned to prison to serve the shortest custodial sentence that he had ever received, a three-month stint after attempting and failing to rob a gun shop.

If you go looking for evil in Miller's history before that moment, it is hard to find. He seemed to operate off a kind of egalitarian morality. Robbing those more fortunate than him to ensure his own survival. His time in jail was never enjoyable, but the prison system fulfilled the same purpose in keeping him alive that his life of crime did on the outside. In prison, he was guaranteed food and some degree of comfort. He was sometimes even able to work, which he genuinely seemed to enjoy. He had no skills, education, or understanding of the systems that would allow him to build a stable life for himself outside of institutional settings, and there was no safety net for people like him in Australia at the time. It would be fair to say that at any given time, a significant portion of the prison population in Australia was made up of people just like James Miller—lost people with no hope for the future just doing their best to survive. Unfortunately, the other significant part of the prison population was made up of people like James' new cellmate, Christopher Robin Worrell.

Chris swept into James' life like a storm. James first spotted the much younger man across the remand yard on the first day that he arrived in jail. Chris stood out from the crowd. He was slim, only twenty years old, smooth skinned, handsome, and pale. He had long luxurious black hair and a happy-go-lucky grin in almost every situation. His constantly upbeat attitude ran completely contrary to Miller's melancholy demeanour, and it was instantly appealing, a little patch of sunshine in the grim grey expanse of the prison yard. Like so many before and after him, James fell for the bad boy.

To be considered a "bad boy" in a jail filled with murderers and maniacs would be quite the feat for anyone who wasn't a violent psychopath. Luckily for Christopher, that was exactly what he was. His psychopathic tendencies were pronounced by the time that he committed his latest crime. His arrest was for the violent rape of a young woman while he was still out on parole for committing an armed robbery a few years prior to the latest atrocity.

James' obsession was immediate and painfully obvious to everyone. Chris noticed the older man's interest, and while he may not have understood the sexual undertones to that interest immediately, he felt no hesitation in helping the friendship to blossom. When James approached him to ask him to be his partner in a game of table tennis, the two began talking. To all appearances, Chris held nothing back in their conversations, cheerfully talking about his time serving in the Royal Australian Air Force in exactly the same tones as he talked about his father's early death and the subsequent arrival of a stepfather whom he never really cared for. Sadly, it is impossible to know exactly where the truth ended and Worrell's own "spin" on reality began. Like all psychopaths, he lied with a casual ease, projecting whatever personality and emotions he believed would serve him best in any given situation. Regardless, the two of them became cellmates within a week and spent almost every waking moment together prior to their trial dates.

Chris' chipper and charming persona was so powerful that James initially thought that the rape charge levelled against him was some sort of joke. Chris had a habit of pulling practical jokes on his cellmate anyway, and this sort of humour seemed to be right in line with the edge of cruelty hidden inside many of his pranks. More than that, though,

James just couldn't understand why someone as charming, nice, and physically attractive as Chris would ever have to rape someone. For his part, Chris tried to play the whole thing off as a misunderstanding to his new friend, explaining that he had far too much to drink to even remember the night in question. He told James that he expected the case to be thrown out when it was discovered that the encounter was completely consensual and the girl had simply been drinking too heavily to remember enjoying herself.

The judge disagreed with that assessment. During his trial, the judge proclaimed him to be "a depraved and disgusting human being," and it is difficult to look at the list of his crimes and disagree. Chris's drinking story fell apart upon closer examination. His victim had been a teenaged hitchhiker whom he attacked in his car. It seems at least moderately unlikely that he was both blackout drunk and driving safely. In addition to the maximum sentence of four years for the rape, he was sentenced to continue a suspended two-year sentence from the armed robbery that had last landed him in jail. Both men were transferred to Yatala Labour Prison to serve out their respective sentences.

Once they were in Yatala, their time was more strictly regimented and their sleeping arrangements were dictated by the administration rather than by the preferences of the prisoners. Even so, they went on spending all of their social time together. From a tactical standpoint, Chris was glad to have a bigger and more experienced inmate on his side. Despite James' effeminate mannerisms, he still struck a more imposing figure than the slender young Chris. While James was never the life of the party, he seemed to relax and become more content the longer he spent with Chris. He did not push the younger man into any sort of sexual contact during their time together in prison. In fact, it seems that even then he immediately slipped into a submissive role towards his friend, following his lead in all things. For a while, it seemed that they would go on playing cards and be joking together forever, but then inevitable tragedy struck. James' brief sentence was completed in only a few short months, and he was cast back out into the world outside, leaving Chris alone.

James' affection for Chris did not wane with the impediment of a prison wall between them. He was despondent outside of prison, and whether he deliberately got himself caught or if his depression prevented him from taking the necessary steps to make his latest criminal enterprise a success, he was soon back in front of the courts. Along with an accomplice, he had stolen over four thousand pairs of sunglasses and was running a business of selling them in hotel bars around Adelaide. Given the repeated nature of his infractions and the value of goods stolen, he managed to secure himself an eighteen-month sentence this time and found himself delivered back to Yatala promptly. Worrell welcomed him back to prison with open arms. They spent the following year and a half together in the closest thing to a stable and structured environment that either man would ever experience. Prison isn't a place where most people can find contentment, but for James, it was a place of safety and security. For a psychopath like Chris, one place was pretty much the same as another. He preferred to be free because it gave him more options for entertainment, but he felt no emotional toll from imprisonment. At the end of the nine months that he actually served of his sentence, James was exiled from the prison once again and returned, despondent, to live with his sister, her husband, and their children. It seemed almost inevitable that he would re-offend in an attempt to return to his beloved Christopher, and his family could see that he was growing more and more restless and miserable as time went by. Then, after only nine months, his luck turned around. Due to prison overcrowding and his exemplary behaviour while behind bars, Chris's sentence was commuted, just as his previous one had been. Finally, the two of them were free to start their life together.

Playing House

Miller often lived with his sister and her family when he was trying to stay on the straight and narrow. She had two daughters who got on well with their uncle despite his frequent disappearances, and even her husband seemed to acknowledge that James was fundamentally harmless. When he was released, he made his way straight there and was welcomed in. Both the children and adults were charmed by the clever and warm young man who had just arrived on their doorstep, and were more than a little relieved to see James finally brightening up after his long slump into depression. For James' sister's husband, he brought another very positive prospect along with him: the promise that their longstanding tenant might finally be moving out.

While they were in prison, the two men had made plans to find an apartment together once they had gathered together enough money. To that end, the two of them both sought out employment immediately. Chris already had a steady job with the white goods manufacturer Simpson Pope, and it didn't take long before James picked up a job of his own working in a dry cleaner's shop. Both men started to save up the deposit that they would need for an apartment, but their habit of going out for a drink together every night after work limited their ability to set aside much. As James had predicted, Chris never had any trouble attracting female attention during their bar crawls, and most nights ended with the younger man heading off to spend the night with his latest conquest and James skulking off home alone.

Drinking and sex seemed to be Chris's primary motivations, with everything else merely being a prelude to, or requirement of, those two actions. He lasted only a few months at the dry cleaner's shop before the repetition and boredom began to take their toll. He quit on the spur of the moment but was lucky enough to land another job with the Unley Council's roadwork gang immediately. Shortly afterwards, he invited Miller to join the crew, too, so that they could spend more time together.

It is impossible to say how much of the friendship between James and Chris was genuine and how much of it was manipulation. There is little doubt that James' intention towards Chris was genuine, even if they were tinged with a desire for romance that Chris seemed willfully unaware of, but whether a psychopath with no empathy whatsoever can even feel affection is another question entirely. For James, this was the happiest time in his life. He got to spend every waking moment with the man he loved, and he had steady work and a safe home to go back to at the end of each night. It probably seemed like he was getting his life on track for the very first time and that Chris was the source of all of this newfound good fortune.

The only point of contention between the two men was the way that Chris insisted they spend their days off touring the sex shops of Adelaide in search of magazines and pornographic materials that appealed to his predilections. Specifically, material revolving around bondage, sadism, and domination. Worrell's personal favourites involved both rape fantasies and complex rope bondage. James was aware of his own sexuality and had learned over the years in prisons and in day to day life in Australia in the 60s that it was unwise to draw attention to who he was, so every time that they visited a sex shop together, he was intensely uncomfortable. Chris either found his discomfort amusing or considered it to be irrelevant, so he went on dragging James around the few stores that sold the kind of material he was looking for. If James had realised at the time that this humiliation was a type of foreplay for Worrell, then he might have been more receptive to it. After finding the magazines that most appealed to him, Chris would head back home with James and masturbate in front of the older man. Miller remained painfully submissive throughout the whole experience, never voicing his own desires, never moving to do anything that might jeopardise his relationship with Chris, just watching and savouring every moment. Eventually, Worrell took the next step, forcefully demanding that James orally stimulate him while he read his magazines. He did not have to ask twice. Bondage and sadomasochism are hardly modern concepts, but before the advent of the internet it was considerably more difficult for enthusiasts to contact each other. The modern codification of BDSM into a "scene" where word-of-mouth offers the participants some measure of protection from dangerous outsiders is also a relatively new. While the holy trinity of modern BDSM is "safe, sane, and consensual," most of the magazines that were published in the 70s played directly to the readers' darkest fantasies without making a stop at any of those three stations. Sex education in the 70s was left mostly to parents, and even if any particularly progressive parent decided to explain bondage to their child, that parent certainly was not Chris Worrell's. Everything that he knew about BDSM came from reading the fetishized accounts in magazines, and his belief that these stories represented real, normal relationships was formative to his view of women. In the rape fantasies that he liked to read, the women would come to love their attacker for the pleasure and pain that they received. This was how Chris Worrell viewed the world and women in particular. For the average person, one who grew up surrounded by people in healthy relationships and who did not have the emotional void that Chris experienced, there would have been balancing factors that would have revealed that this worldview was unrealistic at best, but Chris was the perfect storm of bad information and a supreme willingness to act on it. His relationship with Miller was entirely one-sided. Miller gave him everything and anything that he wanted without anything in return. To Worrell, this made perfect sense, he was dominant and James was his submissive, which meant that his needs and desires were paramount. If you speak to anyone in the modern BDSM community, they will tell you that while the desires of a dominant and a submissive are different, the relationship is still equal, with both having their needs met. There is very little evidence that Miller took any pleasure in submitting to Worrell, but he was so desperate for any sort of relationship that he would do anything to be involved sexually with Chris— no matter how painful or degrading it was. He didn't take pleasure from the pain. He didn't take pleasure from the degradation. He endured them so that he could get to his goal. For several months, they fell into this routine before one day, almost on a whim, Worrell called it off. He still had James tour sex shops with him, but he cut him out of the actual act itself. When James finally got the courage together to ask about it, Chris claimed that he had no interest in men, only women, and that Miller should get over it or move on. That he wanted the two of them to be "like brothers" again. This may have been the truth or it may have just been the latest in the long stream of sexual humiliations that Worrell seemed to delight in inflicting on his love-struck follower. It would be a fitting end to the cycle of abuse that Chris found so pleasurable to offer James the thing that he wanted most in the world and then snatch it away without explanation.

Miller did not see it in those terms. He was smitten with Worrell, through and through, and whether he lied to himself that Chris would one day come around to his way of thinking or whether he genuinely believed that spending platonic time with the love of his life was better than being alone, he settled back into their old routine. Chris maintained the same chipper façade that had carried him through most of their relationship, but now it would occasionally slip and let a hint of his vicious nature shine through. He would complain of headaches, then fall into a foul mood, telling James to go away and leave him alone. At last, Miller began to realise the personality problems that had landed Worrell in prison with him to start with were not all in the mind of the prosecutors. He did his best to calm Chris when he was in his dark moods, keeping him away from populated places where he might act out or hurt others and land himself back in jail.

They steered mostly clear of criminal endeavours because of the terms of their parole, helping out occasionally to move fenced goods from one friend to another without ever truly diving off the deep end in their pursuit of quick cash. However, Chris quickly realised that there was an untapped resource that with James' help they would suddenly be able to access. Now that he knew for certain that Miller was gay and that he hadn't merely been misunderstanding the older man's odd mannerisms, he had James take him to the few gay bars and nightclubs around Adelaide. The two of them would work together to pick up older, wealthier men and bring them back to Chris' apartment where they would rob them of their cash and kick them out with the threat of exposing them as homosexual to the whole world if they tried to report it to the police. These simple robberies were so successful that soon they were banned from every gay club in the city.

When it finally seemed like they were on track to having enough money to get an apartment together, Chris convinced James to spend it on a car instead. They purchased a 1969 Valiant Sedan and spent their time off work cruising around town trawling for girls. This was hardly a new experience for Miller. Ever since they started visiting bars, he had been used as a wingman and a prop to show how safe his friend was to all of the women who he was trying to seduce, but now he had to be present for the latter stages of the seduction. Chris would use the newly purchased car to pick up girls on the street with James acting as his chauffeur and de facto chaperone to convince the girls of their good intentions. Miller would drive them to a secluded location while maintaining amicable silence as the love of his life went through the motions of talking yet another girl into sleeping with him in the back seat, then James would hop out of the car and take a long walk while waiting for the lovers to finish up. With everyone back in their clothes and more or less satisfied, he would then taxi the girls to wherever they wanted to go, and the cycle would start all over again.

The car brought new opportunities to their shakedown scam, too. Although they weren't allowed into any of the gay bars and clubs, there was nothing stopping them from driving by and picking up the men outside. Millers' ability to instinctively spot what Chris called "his own kind" made the whole process very simple and helped them to avoid the few undercover police who were trying to infiltrate the community. They continued to pick up men on and off over the next few months until Worrell gradually lost interest in it. Even though it was still earning them a decent amount of money, he had more interesting things to pursue now that their mobile love-seat was available to him.

James liked to fantasise that one day they would actually go through with what they promised these men to get them into the car. For a supposed heterosexual, Chris had a filthy mouth to match an even filthier imagination. Most of the men that they were picking up off the street would have been satisfied with a quick fumble in the back of the car, but the things that

Chris offered them would have been enough to tempt a saint. Miller probably would have done all right picking up most of these men on his own, despite the way that he assumed he was unattractive, but once they saw the youthful beauty of Chris and heard the obscenities that he offered up casually they couldn't get the car door open fast enough. It wasn't to be, though—the only person to ever have sex in the Valiant was Chris, and it definitely wasn't with James or any other man for that matter.

In the beginning, Worrell's romantic liaisons only happened once or twice a month, but soon Worrell's needs began to escalate. It became every week, then every day. They left work and immediately started a tour of the biggest hotels in town, the bus station, and the train station, looking for women who would like a lift. Eventually, they picked up a girl who decided that she did not want to go through with Chris's idea of a date, and he raped her. James was able to calm the girl on his return to the car and even convinced her not to press charges, citing the usual victim-blaming line that "she knew what she was getting in the car for." After dropping the girl off, Worrell slipped into a black mood that all of Miller's coaxing couldn't draw him back out of. He demanded to be left alone and, slightly shaken by the events of the night, James obliged him. The very next morning, Chris was back to his usual bright and sparkling self when he arrived for their morning shift with the work crew, giving a casual apology for the way that their evening had gone awry and joking that he hoped that this night's hunting trip for a new "rag" would go more smoothly. They returned to their usual routine without delay. James wrote the terrible event off as just an unfortunate misunderstanding, and Chris didn't even bother to comment on it. His next few attempts at seduction were successful, but he still had traces of his dark mood lingering around him afterwards. Regular "vanilla" sex had never really satisfied his needs, and he often brought a rope along to bind his dates with, to increase his own thrill. While Miller would never admit it later in his life, it seems more than likely that his sexual escapades with Chris also involved at least some degree of rope-play as well as the obvious power imbalance that Chris was so happy to exploit for his own gratification.

James eventually settled on a justification for Chris's foul moods that could now last for hours at a time. He believed that there was some sort of physical defect in Chris's brain that was causing these outbursts. That his sociopathic behaviour was something like epilepsy. Violent outbursts that were outside of his control. It gave James the perfect moral justification to ignore anything that Chris ever did when he was in one of his dark moods. After all, if he was ill then it wasn't his fault. James had met plenty of mentally ill people during his time in prison, and while the legal system may not have recognised their diminished responsibility, the people who spent time with them on a daily basis did.

The timeline of Chris's next rapes is a little fuzzy, but they seem to have happened with increasing regularity. Miller continued to disregard them as unfortunate misunderstandings, even going so far as to question the sanity of any girl who would turn his beloved Chris down. Even the consensual encounters took on an increasingly violent edge as Chris tried to pursue the same high that he had experienced during his violent rapes. The sex, which he had always pursued, became secondary to the feelings of domination and the exertion of power over his victims. In terms of psychology, rape is almost never about sex and almost always about power. It is difficult to believe that Christopher Worrell would have had any difficulty committing his crimes alone given his past form and habits, so James' presence at the scene of the crimes seems to be another aspect of the ritual that Worrell was building. The man who wanted him, denied at every turn and forced to watch a parade of other lovers going by. Still, try as he might to keep himself excited, the thrill was fading with each night. First sex wasn't enough. Then bondage wasn't enough. Then rape wasn't enough. All of his violent and sexual passions had intermingled, and with no empathy to hold him back, Christopher Worrell was on a collision course with the inevitable. It was just a matter of time.

Veronica Knight

James wasn't used to the lights. The press of bodies reminded him of prison, the oppressive heat of December was nothing new, and the distant music piping out of the stores reminded him of the car's radio when he went for one of his walks late at night, but the lights were a new experience. The reformatory had never celebrated Christmas, prisons couldn't string up twinkling strings of lights in case they were used as garrotes, and while his sister dragged out her own fairy lights every year that he was visiting them, those tiny little flickers of colour couldn't compare to the dazzling sea of lights that enveloped the streets of Adelaide. Bars used a single string of these lights to brighten up their outdoor seating, but it was nothing compared to this. This was dazzling. Beneath his moustache, shielded from the passing shoppers, James was grinning. He met Chris's eyes over the head of a bustling old woman, and for a moment his breath caught. The sparkle was back, as bright as any Christmas lights. Chris had taken badly to this summer's heat and humidity, joking that he was sweating like he was in front of a jury. He already wore as little as he possibly could while still getting service, so the only thing that he could sacrifice was his hair. It had been trimmed short and parted to the side, the tips of his fringe brushing by his right eye and forcing James to resist the urge to brush it away almost constantly. With the long hair, Chris had looked like a handsome boy, like a hippy or one of the surfers down at the beach, although James didn't think he had ever seen him near the water. Now he looked every inch a man. Even if the perfect symmetry of his features hadn't changed at all, you could see it clearly now. With a wild grin on his face as they pushed through the crowds doing their last-minute shopping, James could almost imagine that he was smiling because of him.

He had barely been able to contain his relief when Chris asked him to come out shopping with him instead of the usual hunt for a new rag. It wasn't that he was jealous. Of course it wasn't that he was jealous. They were only friends after all. Chris had made that perfectly clear. If James wanted to spend time together, then it had to be as friends. He wasn't allowed to think about Chris as anything more than a friend or remember those perfect breathless moments on his knees in front of Chris's chair when he could feel his whole life opening out in front of him. He blinked the treasured memories away before flashing Chris a smile of his own. This wasn't so bad. He could still imagine that they were here together. Really together. That wasn't much different from the truth. They still spent every moment in each other's company. They still planned on getting a house together and spending their lives together. What was kissing compared to all of that? What was sex compared to getting to look into Chris's eyes every single day and know in his gut that this was forever? This was good. Just going out and doing normal things that normal friends do together was good. The fact that he didn't want to spend his nights driving around looking for some silly girl for Chris to screw in the backseat of the car wasn't anything to do with wishing Chris would take him into the backseat of the car—it was because he didn't want to waste his Christmas Eve on something so tawdry. Or it was because he had no interest in chasing after girls? It might even be because it had been a few days since one of Chris's dark moods and he didn't want to see another one of them come on just because some silly bitch didn't know how lucky she was getting.

They hadn't bought anything all night, just wandered the streets and enjoyed the atmosphere and laughed out loud at the clothes store that had sprayed fake snow on its windows like they were on the other side of the world. Chris hadn't stopped laughing and smiling since they got into town, and it was infectious. Everywhere that they went people were smiling back at them, bubbling over with season's greetings and excitement for the next day. James couldn't remember Christmas when he was a kid, but this is what he imagined it was meant to be like. A kaleidoscope of bright colours, flashing lights, and warm smiles everywhere that you looked. Chris carried a cloud of happiness with him wherever he went. Was it any wonder that James was willing to put up with some little eccentricities in exchange?

Chris let the buoying crowd push him closer to James and then leant in closer still. His hot breath on James' cheek made the hair on the back of his neck stand up. "Let's just give it up for the night, mate. It's been fun but I can't even remember what I was looking for anymore." James chuckled and gave the other man a nod. He didn't like the idea of trying to shout over the murmur of voices all around them. He didn't like the sound of his own voice, particularly when he had to shout over a racket. The car was parked just around the corner, so he pushed off to go and fetch it while Chris stared in through a window at a display of glittering jewellery, probably guessing how much he could get for it. James left him with a grin still firmly in place. Neither of them had needed to boost anything to get by since the last time they were in jail, but some instincts never leave you. Even if you want them to.

He drew the Valiant out of its spot in the packed Harris Scarfe car park and rolled around the corner, expecting to find Chris still adding up the value of all the gold in the window, but he was nowhere to be seen. It was a busy street on a busy night, so he didn't worry, but there was a prickle between his shoulder blades that just wouldn't quit. Like a drop of sweat or a mosquito. Something felt wrong, but something always felt wrong to James. He had spent his entire life with that sensation of wrongness clinging to him, following him from place to place and making him flinch away from all the smiling happy people like the ones streaming by his car on the sidewalk. Chris had brought him into the world, made him feel like he belonged there for as long as they were together. James didn't know how he could ever thank him enough. He rolled around the block three times before he spotted Chris on the footpath. He had his back to the road and he was talking to some girl. James groaned. Just when it looked like he was going to get a night without worrying, Chris had spotted some lost little lamb. He swallowed down his resentment and plastered on his best smile before pulling up to the kerb. Maybe he had found them quick enough. Maybe Chris hadn't had time to work his magic on her yet. James could see the Christmas lights shining off her teeth and her wide eyes; it was already too late. She loved him. Sometimes it happened like that. Two minutes was all that it took Chris to make anyone fall for him.

The girl clambered into the back seat and Chris slid into his accustomed spot in the front, crackling with so much energy that James was surprised that he hadn't shorted out the car. He smirked. "This is Veronica. I told her that we were going to show her the hills up by Adelaide. But we've got to get her back in time for her curfew. Don't want her getting in any trouble. Think that we can go for a drive and get her home in two hours, James?"

She still hadn't fastened her belt and she was looking at James in the rearview mirror. Watching his eyes. He nodded and tried to force the fake smile to show all the way up his face. "I'm sure we'll get you back in plenty time."

She relaxed back into the seat and they began the journey out of town. After a moment of their usual amicable silence Veronica blurted out, "Thanks for the ride. I was out shopping with my friend but I got turned around. No idea where she's gone at all."

James actually felt a little twinge of sympathy for her then. She was just a silly girl, lost and alone, going off in a car with two strange men because one of them had a nice smile and the other one seemed safe enough for the both of them. She kept on talking. "Chris here promised me a lift home. Not sure that I should be going off into the hills on Christmas Eve, you know? Busy day in the morning."

James gritted his teeth as Chris did what he always did: insinuated his way around the conversation to make the girl give him whatever he wanted. "It's a beaut' of a night tonight. Be a shame not to make the most of it."

Words were struggling their way up James' throat unbidden. He could end this right now. He could ask the girl where she lived. He could take her home. He could save her from whatever indignities Chris planned to inflict on her in the name of fun. But then Chris would look at him and see right through all of his lies and know why he had done it. He didn't care about this stupid girl. He just wanted her gone so that he could have Chris all to himself. That was the nasty secret that was riding around in this car with them. Not the ready-knotted rope hidden in the glove-box or the dark passions lurking behind Chris' perfect face. That was the truth that could destroy the life that they were building together. James wanted Chris to be more than his friend and Chris wanted him to be obedient and nothing more. He wet his lips and forced out, "It is a beaut' of a night. You two should enjoy yourselves. You're only young once you know. Take it from an old codger." That drew a wicked little giggle from the girl that helped to harden James' resolve. He started off down the dark highway, letting the road markings lead him around the curve in silence. This was what he wanted. He tried to convince himself over and over that this was what he wanted, but the treacherous voice in his heart kept whispering, "You don't want Chris climbing into the backseat with this girl. You want him climbing into the backseat with you. You want Chris to yourself and you are settling for this because you are the saddest coward to ever walk the earth."

Chris nudged him out of his reverie. "Take the road off there."

It was little more than a dirt track out into the middle of nowhere. They had left the sparkling lights of Christmas behind long ago, but now the normal lights of civilisation started to fade, too. Before long, only the lights of nature, and the car's headlights were left. Chris gave him a wink, so he pulled off to the side of the road and muttered, "Would you look at that view?"

He turned to Veronica and Chris but they were already otherwise occupied. Chris was leaning over the back of the seat to kiss her. The wet sounds of their lips filled the car, undercut only by the girl's throaty moaning. James mumbled, "I'm just going for a little walk. Don't mind me."

Then he got out of the car as fast as he could. He didn't want to see what they were doing in there. He didn't want to hear it. It was bad enough that he would have to smell it as he was driving the girl home. He walked off along the dirt road for as far as it would take him, then he went jogging along a rabbit trail to get even more distance from the car. He was sure that he wouldn't hear anything from this distance, but it was so damned quiet out here in the dark that his own thumping heart echoed in his ears and it was easy to mistake that sound for another rhythmic beat that kept on growing in tempo. James slumped down at the foot of a tree and pressed the heels of his hands into his eyes. He just wanted to have one nice night with his boy... with his friend. One night without the impending sense of doom. Without that itch between his shoulder blades or the throb of worry behind his eyes.

At least he had plenty of practice at waiting alone in the dark, both from his criminal days and far too many nights of doing exactly what he was doing now. Standing in the cupboard had been a punishment back home before he left, and "isolation" was standard practice in the reformatory when you were indulging in "sinful practices." As far as James had been able to tell, sinful practices included absolutely anything that a teenage boy locked in a dormitory with a hundred other teenage boys might want to do, so he spent a lot of his youth waiting alone in little dark rooms. If his family had been Catholic it might have reminded him of a confessional. It might have been a place for him to clear his guilty conscience and walk back into the light feeling clean, but he wasn't that lucky. He had nowhere to put his guilt but to push it down inside his head and wait for it to bubble up when he had a quiet moment alone. Just like this one. His time in isolation and his time in the cupboard back home were meant to be spent reflecting on his wicked ways and, in a sense, James had made good use of it for that. He had planned out nearly all of his crimes sitting alone in dark places with nobody to bother him. Introspection wasn't a smart choice for a career criminal, but James wasn't very good at making smart choices, as the current situation proved. When he had these moments to himself, when Chris was busy with his latest rag, he thought about his life. He thought about the places he had been and the things he had seen. He thought about the things that he would do tomorrow and the next day. In short, he thought about anything that he could to escape from what was happening right now. It had served him well back when he was being punished, this ability to cast his mind out in search of the greener pastures he had already passed by or the ones that he would be coming upon soon. Right now, he had no idea what he was doing. He had no idea what the future was going to hold. It should have terrified him, that loss of control, that abandonment of the careful planning that he had used throughout his life to keep his sanity, but instead, he found himself strangely relaxed. He could trust in Chris to guide him through. Chris wouldn't worry and fret. He probably wouldn't plot and plan, either. He would take each day as it came and announce to the world what he wanted from it. James wished that he had the knack of doing that, because nine times out of ten, whatever Chris wanted he ended up getting sooner or later. It wasn't that he was lucky or that he was smart, he just set his feet on the ground, looked the whole universe in the face and waited for it to flinch first. It went beyond confidence into an almost supernatural power, and it led to James waiting out here on a tree while Chris had sex back in the car every night that he chose to.

In the beginning, he had no idea how long Chris would take with a girl. He deliberately maintained his ignorance as far as sex with women went. He wasn't repulsed or appalled like people claimed to be about the idea of sex with a man, but he just didn't see the appeal even slightly. Still, after a couple of times coming back to the car a little too early and catching a glimpse of pale flesh through the window, he now erred on the side of caution. It was bad enough that it was happening, in his car, he didn't need to see it happening, too. This time he left it even longer than usual, an unusual rebellious streak bubbling up from his anxiety. Maybe Chris could wait on him for once. Except of course, Chris wouldn't wait. If James took too long then he would just hop over into the driver's seat and head home, leaving his best friend stranded in the wilderness. It wasn't viciousness or cruelty—it was just Chris's nature. He would just assume that James had found something better to do and move on with his life. It would be easy for him because he didn't love James. Chris didn't really love anyone, except for himself. Even telling himself that wasn't enough to break the spell, though. James could tell himself a million terrible things about Chris and, at the end of the day, his devotion still wasn't going to fade away. The heart didn't respond to facts. He loved James with the same desperate draw that stopped him from drifting off into space, and the fact that the man didn't love him back, or was too messed up to admit that he loved him back, was irrelevant to the forces that were at work. James watched a few tiny puffs of cloud drifting across the moon. He listened to the distant sound of the Kookaburras laughing in the distant trees. He drew in deep breaths of the summer air. He did literally anything that he could think of to distract himself from what he knew was going on in the car and what he feared was going on in the car. He waited for as long as he felt that he could wait. Until he was certain that Chris was on the verge of starting up the car and driving off without him. Then he started his slow trudge back to the car.

Chris was sitting in the front seat, staring blankly ahead. The windows were wound down but there was no music playing on the radio. The quiet of the night seemed unnaturally exaggerated without the crackle of the radio or the hum of the car's engine. The girl was nowhere to be seen. James crept closer, the sense of wrongness building with every step. Where was the girl? Had Chris done it again? Chris didn't move, although he must have seen James approaching. Eventually, when he felt like the weight of the hot silent air on him was going to crush him, James whispered, "Where's Veronica?"

Chris didn't look at him, but James could already tell that one of his black moods was on him. His brows were drawn down and his breathing was irregular. His voice had none of its usual bounce and joy when he snapped, "She's in the back. On the floor."

James leant over him to peer through the gap in the seats, and there she was. A glimpse of pale flesh in the moonlight, red welts raised on the bare skin by the rough rope. James gasped, "What happened?"

Chris still wouldn't look at him. He answered calmly, "I killed her."

Inside, James was screaming. Without his permission, his hand seized the front of Chris' shirt. Chris grabbed his wrists and pulled himself free with a jerk. He pushed James back as he got out of the car and the two men stood face to face in the moonlight. James wailed, "Why? What did you do it for? Why?"

In the moonlight, he saw the shimmer of the long knife in Chris' hand. He didn't even know that the man had a knife. Chris whispered, "I will kill you, too. Do you hear me? If you don't lay off, I will kill you, too."

James backed away from Chris, desperately trying to force his thoughts into some sort of order. His hands were shaking and he felt that weakness creeping down into his legs, too. He stalked around to the driver's seat and slumped in. Chris slipped back into his own seat without a word, secreting the knife somewhere about his person.

With nothing else to do, James started the engine. The car's headlights came back to life, illuminating the scrub and the gentle slopes ahead of them. Chris spoke so softly that James had to lean closer to hear him. "Don't ask me why I killed her. I don't know myself."

James looked into his eyes and tried to find any hint of remorse. He tried to convince himself that it wasn't Chris. Not his Chris. Not really. It was the black moods. It was the evil seizure inside his brain that had made him choke the life out of some young girl in the backseat of the car. James mumbled, "What—what do we do?"

Chris settled back into his seat. "Drive out to Gawler."

With no better ideas and a brain frozen with shock, James put the car into gear and pulled back onto the dirt track.

Without Veronica's constant prattle, they brought the deathly silence of the hillside along with them inside the car. Chris, who usually found words so easily, tried to fill it with a dull monotone. "I'd kill my own mother if I thought she'd put me on."

James didn't know what to say to that. He had never really been afraid of Chris before. He knew the man had a violent streak—he had seen it first hand more than a few times—but it had always been something that he had tried to shield the rest of the world from, to keep Chris safe and free. He had never even considered that Chris might hurt him. Break his heart, yes. Abandon him, yes. Lose interest, most definitely. But the thought that Chris might turn around and try to kill him was just ludicrous. James tried to keep his eyes on the road, but his eyes kept on getting dragged back to the girl in the back. Murder was a common word back in prison, and violence was commonplace, but this was still the first time that James had seen a dead body. He supposed that he had lived a sheltered life in his way. She didn't look dead. Not yet. Not like the dead bodies in movies. She just looked like she was sleeping really soundly. With her eyes open. The car started to drift out of its lane until Chris gave him a nudge with his elbow and he started paying attention to where he was going again.

They drove out past the little township of Truro, far from Adelaide and the watchful eyes of a big city. Chris barked at him to stop when they had reached a desolate enough spot by a copse of trees. More than anything, James desperately did not want to touch the dead girl, but when he hesitated Chris snarled at him and reached as if he were going for his knife again. James took a grip on the rope that bound her wrists together and closed his eyes, and together they dragged her out onto the dirt. After a few minutes of fumbling in the trunk of the car, they discovered that they didn't have a shovel, and a hint of Chris crept back into his voice as he sniggered. They laid the girl down on the ground and covered her with branches. Then they drove away.

James didn't stop shaking as they drove away, and now that a little spark of energy had come back to Chris it was almost worse than when he was sitting and staring dead-eyed out into the night. Chris never shut up at the best of times and now, with the black mood rooted deeply and some grim spark of energy returning, he started to talk. "Was that your first one? Never seen somebody die before? I've seen plenty."

He twisted in his seat to stare at the side of James' head. Sweat was pouring off of the older man from the heat, the exertions, and the new fear that he found gnawing at his guts. "I saw a boy drown. When I was just a kid. He was my friend. We were out swimming in the sea and I watched him drown and didn't lift a finger to help him. I just watched."

James didn't say anything. He didn't know why Chris was telling him this. It was bad enough that he had killed that girl in one of his frenzies, but what he was describing, that wasn't a temper run riot—it was cold-blooded, calculating. That wasn't the Chris that he knew at all. Even at his worst, all you had to worry about with Chris was his temper. James wondered if this was Chris trying to give him fair warning about the price of their friendship. He imagined what it would be like, to die like that, expecting Chris to save you at any moment. He imagined what it would be like to die like that stupid girl Veronica, too. To feel Chris on top of you, feel all of his heat and weight bearing down on you and crushing the air out of you. James let out a little-strangled sound and a tear ran down his cheek. He was jealous of a dead girl. If it hadn't been so pathetic it would have been funny.

Chris was still staring at him. Watching him cry and shake with a silent curiosity that reminded James of a snake watching a mouse. Chris leant a little closer across the gap between their chairs, and that simple movement that would have filled James with happiness earlier in the night made him freeze with fear. There was heat creeping back into Chris's voice now, the same heat that James could remember from those sweaty days reading his dirty magazines in his boarding house room. Despite himself, James shivered. "That wasn't my last dead body. You know that already right? Back when I was in the Air Force, running down from Perth to Adelaide on leave, I picked up a hitchhiker. A girl. Cute little thing. I knifed her. It was so messy. Blood squirting out everywhere. I'd hate to kill somebody like that again. Took me days to get the car clean."

James wet his lips. It didn't matter that the things that Chris was saying were terrible. All that mattered was his voice. James whispered, "And?"

Chris's dead face cracked into a smile now that he knew that he had his audience on the hook. A flicker of light came back into his eyes. "She was the first one, but she wasn't the last. Plenty of hitchhikers between the base and town. The next girl, I wasn't daft enough to use the knife again. I bashed her head in with a rock instead. That was a lot more fun."

He was close enough that his breath was tickling James' ear. Close enough to kiss. He whispered, "So you know that I'll have no problem doing you if you say a single word about this to anyone. I don't want to speak about tonight. Not now. Not ever again. Do you understand me?"

James nodded carefully and Chris's smile slipped away again. "Take me home, James. I'm tired and it's about five minutes until Christmas."

Tania Kenny

Over the Christmas break, James was distraught, but he maintained his vow of silence, sitting through Christmas dinner with his sister's family with little more than a flicker of interest when the kids tried to play with their favourite uncle. He couldn't integrate the idea of his friend Chris, the love of his life, being a killer. His violent streak and dark moods had always been a distant threat, a tiny aberration from the sweetness and kindness of Chris's usual personality. The idea that the viciousness and cruelty that had appeared in glimpses through the years were an integral part of him, rather than the affliction that he had assumed it was, chilled him. He had trouble sleeping, completely failing to find any rest the first night and waking fitfully all through the night of Christmas itself when exhaustion finally overtook him.

He saw Chris the next day when they returned to work and, to his utter amazement, the man was back to acting exactly the same way that he always had before. Smiling and joking around with James and his coworkers in equal measure despite the sweltering heat. It made the horror of Christmas Eve feel like a dream, like a mistake, like James was just confused about the whole thing. It might have been worse than that sickening dread he had been feeling over the last two days. Before, James had been struggling to reconcile the happy-go-lucky life of the party with the acts of brutality that Chris had committed, but now he was confronted with the terrible truth that he didn't care. It didn't matter that Chris was a killer any more than it had mattered when he was a rapist or a thief or any of the other terrible things that they had both been at various points in their lives. James loved him, and it only took a few moments in his company to remind him of that inescapable fact.

For his part, Chris seemed to realise that he had crossed some sort of line and tried to make amends. That night after their work was done, they went out drinking, and his eyes never strayed away from James. Through the whole night he squashed any interest that he might have had in anyone else in the world and made James feel like the centre of it all. Like all clever abusers, he lavished gifts on James in an attempt to tip the scales of affection back in his favour. His first gift was the night of undivided attention, but the second was considerably more substantial. The thing that James had been longing for over the past few months but had never been bold enough to press his friend for. He announced that he had found an apartment for them to share and that they had enough money saved to move in right away. James' sister and her family were in the process of moving to a new house, and while he had intended to tag along, the timing could not have been more perfect for him to move out. As good as his relationship with his sister was, James could still recognise that he was putting a strain on her marriage just by being present. Moving in with Chris was exactly what he had wanted since they first left prison but now, after the events of a few nights ago, he was feeling serious doubts about the decision. Doubts that Chris was happy to wear down with his usual good humour and more casual affection than James had experienced in the last month.

With the agreement made and a night of heavy drinking behind them, Chris skipped out from work briefly the next day to sort out the requisite paperwork. Afterwards, they went out drinking again to celebrate and soon fell into their familiar pattern, with Chris flirting with every girl who moved and James setting him up for his cleverest jokes. Before, there had been a certain pleasure in it for James, knowing that he was helping Chris to get what he wanted. There was satisfaction in it, even if it was very distant from the satisfaction that he would like to have felt with Chris. Now, every flirtation came with a dangerous undertone. Before Christmas, the worst thing that James thought could happen was one of the girls getting cold feet and trying to pin another rape charge on Chris. Something that he was fairly confident that he could talk them out of, if given enough time. Now he knew that there were some things that you couldn't talk your way out of. When Chris went off with a girl at the end of the night, a girl who James had helped to convince to sleep with him, he wondered if she was going to live to see the next morning.

Whether she did or not, Chris was back in top form at work the next day. They fell back into the same routines. They went out hunting for a new girl for Chris each night. James walked away from the car in the dark. If he suspected that the girls were going to be killed, then he never let them know. The time began to flow by again, just as swiftly as it had before. Before he knew it, his sister had moved out of her apartment. Before he knew it, a week had passed since Veronica. His sister's lease still had another week left, so James had plenty of time to go and collect the clothes that he had left behind there before moving into his new apartment. Chris came with him on their day off, and they planned to go out to celebrate some more afterwards. As they were driving through the central business district of Adelaide, Chris had him pull over and stop. He told James to wait for him as he went jogging off into the crowd and, like an obedient servant, James waited for him. It came as no surprise when he returned leading a girl by the hand, his usual charming grin threatening to take over his entire face. The girl, Tania Kenny was only fifteen years old, but Chris had no scruples. She chatted incessantly as they drove, making clumsy attempts at flirtation with Chris that set James' eyes rolling and talking great detail about her studies. She was a bright girl, chatty and happy, having her first adventure into adulthood. When they arrived at James' sister's apartment, Chris put his hand on James' knee and told him to just wait in the car while they fetched his clothes from inside the house. The subtext was so obvious that James just turned off the engine and sighed.

Chris led his teenage girlfriend by the hand into the apartment building and James, after the initial rush of irritation, started to doze in the late morning sunshine. The day dragged on and he kept on waiting until finally, a shadow blocked out the sunlight that had been warming him. He opened his eyes to see Chris looming outside the car. His face expressionless. His voice monotone as he said, "I need your help."

James burst out of the car and rushed into the apartment without a moment's hesitation. He knew what that face meant. What that voice meant. He only hoped that this time he would have time to stop the tragedy before it could come to its conclusion. In one of the empty bedrooms, on the floor, lay Tania Kenny. She was still fully clothed, which James considered to be a blessing, but her hands and feet had been bound with plastic-clad wire and there was a large piece of sticking plaster pasted over her mouth. The medical plaster was already soaked through with red and blood was trickling through it, running down the dead girl's cheek and staining the carpet.

James turned on Chris and started yelling every obscenity that he could think of. Letting all of the pent up fear and hate and fury of the last week pour out in a torrent. Chris, never one to stand idly by when insults were being flung, began berating, belittling, and degrading James right back. The two men screamed back and forth over the top of the dead girl for a solid ten minutes before James started to get hoarse and stopped. Chris said, "Is that you finished?"

James bit back his reply, then nodded to the remains of Tania, "Why?"

Chris shrugged then peered out the window at the street lit up by the midday sun. "Guess we can't get rid of it just now."

"If you don't want to go dragging dead girls out in broad daylight then maybe you should stop making them," James sniped back.

Chris scowled at him, "We've got a problem to deal with here. You want to help or do you want to mouth off?"

James growled, "I'd much rather mouth off than deal with dead bodies."

Chris ignored him. "We'll have to move it tonight. But we can go dig a hole for it now. We've got all day."

James let out a little whine. "We can't leave her there. The landlord could come in or my sister could come back or—we can't leave her there."

Together they got a grip on the dead girl, still warm to the touch, and crammed her into a cupboard, propping it shut with a chair just to be on the safe side.

They drove out to Wingham, on the northern outskirts of Adelaide, and dug a shallow grave for Tania. The familiarity of the labour brought some life back into Chris, who started trying his usual banter with James as they worked. James was silent throughout their digging, staring down into the grave and wondering just how long it was going to be until Chris was digging one of them for him. There had been no more threats or cajoling this time around and, with a nauseating sensation, James realised why. He was already complicit. He had covered up the last murder. He had hidden that girl's body out in the wilderness under a pile of twigs. He was guilty. He did this just as surely as if it were his hands closing on the girl's throat. As a criminal, there was a twisted code of ethics that was frequently discarded whenever personal gain became involved, but the one unbreakable rule was that you did not get the police involved. Chris wasn't with him every moment of every day. If he had wanted to turn him in for the last murder and free himself of all guilt all it would have taken was a phone call or a quick drive down to the police station. He had made his decision. He might have made it the first time that he laid eyes on Chris. He was in for the long haul. Even so, he couldn't bring himself to be a willing participant.

They drove back into town as the sun was setting, wrestled the body of Tania out of the house and into the trunk under cover of darkness, and then returned to the grave in the middle of nowhere. James helped Chris lift the girl out of the car, and he helped lower her into the ground, but he couldn't bring himself to bury her. He crept back to the car and smoked until Chris was done filling the grave. He drove them both home to spend their first night together in their new apartment. His forgotten clothes sat neatly folded on the back seat of the car. A dirty shovel lay across the floorboards.

Juliet Mykyta

Christopher Worrell turned 23 in January of 1977, only a few weeks after killing Tania. There was very little that could be done in the way of celebration, as Chris spent every single day and night doing exactly what he most enjoyed doing and James spent his every waking moment trying to keep Chris happy. After his last dark mood, Chris had snapped back to normal. He had continued to go on "dates" every night without incident and James was starting to convince himself that his friend might actually have returned to his usual self. Once or twice, anxiety had overcome him and James had snuck back to the car early to make sure that everything was going smoothly. Both times, all that he saw were a young couple involved in such deep kissing and heavy petting that they didn't even notice him peering through their windows.

James refused to let go of the idea that there was some sort of medical problem causing Chris's aberrant behaviour, and he frequently dropped hints that he thought Chris should visit a doctor or a psychologist to talk about his black moods and violent outbursts. Chris brushed this all off as unnecessary, claiming that he was fine and that there was nothing to worry about. Eventually, James' wheedling started to put a strain on their relationship until even Chris's amicable façade cracked and he told him to lay off. James noted the outburst, but it passed so quickly that he wasn't even sure if it could be counted as a black mood so much as a man getting annoyed with his friend trying to mother him. Every night that Chris successfully bedded another woman without killing her seemed to add credence to the theory that his bouts of murderous rage were finally at an end. James, so desperate to believe that his friend wasn't a monster to be feared and so very desperate for life to return to normalcy, did what he always did: he shut up and let Chris have his way.

They were out for their usual drive around town when Chris spotted a girl that he liked the look of at a bus stop. He had James pull up at the side of the road while he went to talk to her. James sat behind the wheel, listening to the radio and ignoring all of his doubts with as much vigor as he could muster. It was a sign of how bad things had gotten that he didn't feel even a pang of jealousy towards the girl, only a pang of pity and a deep-seated anxiety. James Miller knew all about fear—it had been the driving force behind most of the decisions that he had made in his life. Fear of pain, fear of rejection, fear of exposure, fear of getting caught. Even much of his relationship with his beloved Chris was characterized by fear. He never pushed Chris to do anything, or to stop doing anything, for fear of driving him away, and now it seemed that his wish had been granted. The two of them were bound together in their guilt now, even if Chris seemed incapable of feeling it. James felt the guilt almost as deeply as he felt the fear of being caught, but it still wasn't enough to overpower his other emotions. He loved Chris as much as he was capable of loving another human being, even if his fear stopped him from ever expressing that love. The key thing about his fear was that it had always been a force driving him forward before this moment. He would steal for fear of starving. He would lie for fear of getting caught. This was the first time in his life that fear had paralyzed him instead of empowering his actions. The first time that he didn't know which way to turn or which direction to run. He was trapped in the web of his own bad decisions, and there was no way out. The girl slipped into the back seat with a wave and a smile. James' stomach turned. She looked even younger than the last one.

She introduced herself shyly as Julie. She had just finished work at her part-time job, and Chris had offered her a lift home. Chris hopped into the car an instant later and began working on her as James drove, deliberately slowly, towards where she wanted to go. After only a few minutes of flirting and cajoling, Chris convinced her that they had time before she was due back to come take a look at the view up by Port Wakefield instead. James said nothing. He just drove where he was told to drive. As they were driving, Chris started to take his ropes out of the glove box. He turned to Julie and asked for her wrists. She was understandably confused. James just drove on. It was hardly the first time that Chris's love life had started to unfold before he made it out of the car. Chris went back to his usual charm offensive, telling her that it would be fun, that she should "try it before she knocked it." But the sheltered 16-year-old had no idea what Chris was talking about. She didn't even know that bondage as a sexual practice existed. Chris continued trying to convince her, but the innocent girl didn't even seem to realize that he had picked her up for sex. Chris became more and more frustrated as the conversation went on, believing that the girl's innocent replies were actually some kind of game that she was playing. By the time that James had pulled off to the side of a dirt road, he had his temper back under control and had switched to a more traditional attempt at seduction, which seemed to be working despite the girl's nervousness. James got out of the car to go for a walk and a smoke and, glancing back, he saw that the couple in the car seemed to be kissing, despite Julie's initial reluctance.

The night air was cooler now than it had been a few weeks back, when all of the madness had first kicked off, and after the scorching heat of the day that James had endured it was a genuine relief. They were just on the outskirts of Adelaide now, not right out in the wilderness where Chris usually liked to take his dates for some peace and quiet. There was a petrol station lit up at the very end of the road. Its neon lights shining in the darkness like a beacon, guiding James along the curve of dirt. He decided to pick up a pack of cigarettes and then head back—that should give Chris enough time to finish up with the girl. He had only made it a short way down the road before he heard a cry of pain from behind him, and the simmering anxiety that had been churning in his guts since the moment he laid eyes on Julie exploded into wild panic. He turned and ran back along the road, tripping and stumbling over the loose rocks at the side. The little obstacles that he could have easily avoided in the daylight had become invisible as night fell. As he came around the bend he could see movement outside the car, two figures tumbling over each other in the dirt. Chris was straddling the girl's body, sitting on her stomach, and his hands were at her throat. Juliet's screams for help were cut short as he tightened his grip and bore down on her. His face was a fixed mask of blind fury. The shrieking fear that drove James' every motion fell silent in the shock of the moment, and he careened into Chris. He grabbed him by the shirt and yelled at him, "Get off her."

But Chris didn't even flinch. He met his only friend's eyes and hissed, "Take your hands off me." James tried to pull Chris away, but his grip on the girl's throat was relentless. Once again, he growled, "Take your hands off me, or you're next."

James staggered back a step, struck by the pure hatred in Chris's eyes. Intellectually, James had understood that Chris was a killer, but seeing him in the throes of it, in the throes of the one great passion in his life, was just too overwhelming. It wasn't just the threat of violence. James had heard enough of those in his lifetime to know when they were a serious warning and when they were bragging. From Chris it was neither—it was just an ice-cold statement of the facts. If James interfered in his murders, then Chris would bring an end to his life. It had a terrible simplicity to it, but also a terrible relief once he had latched onto it. This was the excuse that James needed to morally justify going along with Chris. This was the lie that he could tell others and himself again and again when confronted. He had to go along with Chris or he would be killed. In reality, there were a million ways he could get around it, but in his terror-filled haze it was solid ground for him to stand on. A moral centre that he could use to justify everything else as "survival." He was still shaking, but he let out a sigh of relief.

Beneath Chris, Juliet's body stopped moving. James didn't even try to pull Chris off again. He wasn't strong enough to stop him. Physically, he might have been a good match, but he just didn't have the will to harm his friend, and that was what it would have taken to get Chris to let go of his victim now that he was locked on. Once he was certain that the girl was dead, Chris turned his fury on James for "spoiling it." He verbally abused James as they gathered up Juliet's body and loaded it into the backseat, and only when she was covered with a blanket did the tirade of slurs and spite taper off. James didn't bother to respond. He knew that nothing he said made a blind bit of difference to Chris. Chris would just go on doing whatever he wanted to do for as long as he wanted to go on doing it, and there wasn't a damned thing that anyone could do to stop him.

This time Chris didn't tell him where to drive. He drove out to Truro without a backwards glance or a question. They didn't have a shovel with them this time, and the night was slipping away from them by the moment. Out in the wilderness beyond the rural township of Truro, they dumped the teenager's corpse and covered it in a mound of sticks to match the tiny memorial that they had raised over Veronica Knight only a month ago. Both girls were left to rot in the sun within walking distance of each other. There was no hesitation from James this time. Now that he had found an excuse to cling to, he was free to do what felt natural again. To love, honour, and obey Chris unconditionally, no matter if the orders he received were to pleasure him, drive him around town, or help him cover up his terrible crimes. The time for rebellion was over. James wouldn't be spoiling his fun ever again.

Sylvia Pitman

James might have lost his reluctance, but after the interruption during his killing of Juliet, Chris seemed to have acquired some of his own. He turned cold towards James, with all of his usual gregarious nature turning outside of the relationship towards their mutual friends and acquaintances from work. To them, he probably appeared as upbeat and pleasant as he had always been, but to James, it was like an icicle or knife in the gut every time Chris's smile swept past him without stopping. Chris had accepted him for who he was from the very first moment that they met. He had been as upfront and honest with him as men in their situation could be, and in return, James had betrayed that trust by asking him to change a fundamental part of who he was. The shame that had been hammered into James in his early years started to resurface in the most obscene way possible. He started to feel guilty about stopping Chris from killing.

Their hunting trips were put on a temporary hiatus. They would still go out drinking and they would still take drives around town, but Chris no longer seemed to be looking for women to satisfy his urges. If he hadn't been being so cold towards him, then James might have taken this as a good sign, an indication that maybe Chris could finally see that he had a good thing going with the other man and that he didn't have to go looking further afield for romance. James might have been an eternal optimist, but even he wasn't stupid enough to believe that all of his dreams would come true after he had just ruined one of the few moments of pleasure Chris seemed to find in life. The more that he watched Chris without being on the receiving end of his charm, the more obvious it became to James that the other man was actually relatively joyless. He went through the motions of being happy, he smiled and laughed and messed around with his workmates on the crew, but now that James had seen under the mask, he recognised the deception for what it was. Unfortunately for the women of Australia, James was more of a romantic than a psychologist. He believed that underneath the surface his beloved was a tortured soul, desperate for just a few moments of release that he could only find through committing the terrible acts of violence that he did. He didn't understand that underneath the charming mask of sanity there was nothing but a gaping void where a human being would have had a conscience.

James was starting to suspect that Chris had locked him out of that whole part of his life in response to his latest mistake. That Chris was somehow finding the time in the few hours they weren't together each day to murder and hide a woman. It made no logical sense, but that had never been an inhibitor to fear, so he gradually became more and more clingy, following Chris around even when he had no reason to, or when it impeded his own plans for the day. So it was that he ended up loitering while Chris was going through the usual motions of chatting about his sexual exploits, minus their lethal endings, with their slightly older and more settled workmates who liked to live through him vicariously. This time when pressed for details of his latest "rags," Chris came out with something completely unexpected. He suggested that he was thinking of finding a nice girl and settling down.

James nearly collapsed. He had never planned for the future because all of his past experience had taught him how quickly plans fall apart, but he was emotionally invested in his relationship with Chris, even if the other man had special needs that he wasn't capable of fulfilling, and he had assumed that they were going to go on with their lives in at least a similar way in the future. The idea of Chris leaving him and settling down into some nice normal straight relationship was an even worse nightmare than the idea of Chris murdering women for pleasure. James' sexuality wasn't exactly a secret among his workmates, and if it weren't for Chris's quick wit and protection, the jibes about it may very well have escalated into something more vicious, but even so, he couldn't say anything to Chris about this terrible idea in front of his workmates without appearing like the jealous love-struck homosexual that most of them had already pegged him as. As Chris joked with the men about whether they had any sisters or daughters that they could hook him up with, James' whole world shattered around him.

They left work that day with the message already spreading around their limited social circles in Adelaide that the dashing notorious womaniser Chris Worrell was looking to settle down. James was so used to following Chris and obeying his every whim by this point that he wasn't even able to broach the subject as he drove him into town. They were swinging by the train station when Chris spotted something of interest and came back to life after a full day of acting like Miller wasn't even there. "Pull over! I want that one."

A girl was standing outside of the train station, checking her purse and about to head in. For a moment she looked odd to James' untrained eye. Looking at her from the back she seemed like a middle-aged woman, but the moment he caught a glimpse of her in profile he realised that she was only a teenager, dressed up in clothes that were far too mature and formal for her. It accentuated her youth—she looked like a kid dressed up in her mother's clothes. When Chris closed the distance with her, the similarities continued. You could tell from the way that her eyes were darting around that she was a little nervous being approached by older men, but Worrell played her fear of being treated like a child perfectly to make her feel like turning down a lift and wasting money on a train would be an immature choice. She bought it hook line and sinker. Before even a minute had passed, she slipped into the back seat and, unlike usual, Chris slipped in beside her. She rattled off instructions to Miller as if he was a taxi driver, and for a moment the absurdity of this little girl trying to play-act like an adult almost made him laugh out loud. She had probably never heard adults giving anyone but a taxi driver their address before.

He pulled away from the station and headed out to the area around Windang dump where it was almost guaranteed to be quiet at this time of night. Sylvia was trying to carry the conversation in the back seat, paying no attention to the direction that they were heading, or much of anything else now that Chris was looking right at her. She kept trying for sophistication, never realising just how wasted it was on Worrell, who wouldn't know sophisticated if it had bitten him on the backside. James stayed out of the conversation entirely, happy to play the role of a taxi driver for as long as it took to get him back in Chris's good books and not sure that he would be able to fake his way through an interaction so stupid without breaking down and laughing. Without the distraction of talking, he made good time out of town, and when he pulled up at the side of the road, Chris graced him with only a sideways glance before telling him to take a nice long walk. He turned off the car and did what he was told, stalking off into the night to take a long rest against a tree. He tried to keep his mind clear. He tried not to think about what Chris was doing right now. He must have waited twice as long as he did on a usual night, his mind turning over the last few days' events over and trying to come to some rational explanation. He would do anything for Chris. He had realised that a long time ago, but he had not realised just how expansive "anything" actually was. It encompassed a multitude of sins that until recently James would have said were completely beyond him. The girl dressed up in an adult's clothes would be dead by now. Dead thanks to James' actions just as much as by Chris's. He had to find some way to square that away. Some way to make that all right despite how obviously wrong it was. She was a person before she climbed into his car, a person with hopes and dreams and a future, and he had nothing but Chris. She could have had anything but she wanted the one thing that belonged to him. Anger was unfamiliar to James, but he found that he could muster a low simmer of it when he contorted his thoughts around to this point of view. He wouldn't say that she deserved it. That was too much of a stretch, but if she hadn't been greedy she would still be alive.

It was almost like a fairy tale moral. It was dark and the air was cooling by the time he finally got up and dusted himself off.

Back at the car, he could see Chris's face lit up by his cigarette's orange glow like a beacon guiding him home. There were far worse things to be coming back to than a satisfied Chris, even if the man was scowling at him as though he had done something wrong. As usual. Chris came away from the car when James drew close enough and slapped him across the cheek hard enough to draw an anguished yelp from the older man. He snarled, "If you say one word tonight I swear to you I will dump your worthless corpse out in the desert just like that rag. One word and you're done for. I'm not going to ask twice."

Tears rolled down James' cheeks, stinging the rosy skin on one side, but he nodded dutifully and got into the driver's seat. The girl was laid out under a rug on the back seat, fully dressed and unbound. The only thing that seemed to be missing were the ridiculous pantyhose that she had been wearing. That was until James looked a little closer and realised that they were wrapped tight around her throat.

The pantyhose knotted around her neck were likely the cause of her lovely purple complexion. The girl had looked too young before, now she looked like a baby. Her lips pouted out with a fat dead slug of a tongue protruding between them. Her eyelids were swollen like she had been stung by bees. It was like her entire head was one giant bruise. James stared and stared with the breath caught in his throat. The other girls hadn't looked like this when Chris was done with them. He couldn't even recognise the girl anymore. He doubted that her closest friends or family would know her if she walked down the street looking like that. She looked completely inhuman, like some sort of doll, and that made it easier. She wasn't human, at least not anymore. She hadn't been human since Chris first laid eyes on her—she was a rag. Something to be used up and discarded.

Whatever Chris thought James was about to say, it was enough to make him draw his knife and pat it against his leg in anticipation. James met his gaze unsteadily for a moment, trying to get the roiling in his stomach under control, then he plastered a smile onto his face. He drove them out to Truro like he was meant to, hauled the corpse out into the bush and tossed a few sticks and leaves on top like he was meant to. He did everything that he was meant to and it still didn't seem to be enough. Chris wouldn't even look at him when he got back into the car, although at least the knife had vanished back out of sight once again.

Sylvia Pitman

James might have lost his reluctance, but after the interruption during his killing of Juliet, Chris seemed to have acquired some of his own. He turned cold towards James, with all of his usual gregarious nature turning outside of the relationship towards their mutual friends and acquaintances from work. To them, he probably appeared as upbeat and pleasant as he had always been, but to James, it was like an icicle or knife in the gut every time Chris's smile swept past him without stopping. Chris had accepted him for who he was from the very first moment that they met. He had been as upfront and honest with him as men in their situation could be, and in return, James had betrayed that trust by asking him to change a fundamental part of who he was. The shame that had been hammered into James in his early years started to resurface in the most obscene way possible. He started to feel guilty about stopping Chris from killing.

Their hunting trips were put on a temporary hiatus. They would still go out drinking and they would still take drives around town, but Chris no longer seemed to be looking for women to satisfy his urges. If he hadn't been being so cold towards him, then James might have taken this as a good sign, an indication that maybe Chris could finally see that he had a good thing going with the other man and that he didn't have to go looking further afield for romance. James might have been an eternal optimist, but even he wasn't stupid enough to believe that all of his dreams would come true after he had just ruined one of the few moments of pleasure Chris seemed to find in life. The more that he watched Chris without being on the receiving end of his charm, the more obvious it became to James that the other man was actually relatively joyless. He went through the motions of being happy, he smiled and laughed and messed around with his workmates on the crew, but now that James had seen under the mask, he recognised the deception for what it was. Unfortunately for the women of Australia, James was more of a romantic than a psychologist. He believed that underneath the surface his beloved was a tortured soul, desperate for just a few moments of release that he could only find through committing the terrible acts of violence that he did. He didn't understand that underneath the charming mask of sanity there was nothing but a gaping void where a human being would have had a conscience.

James was starting to suspect that Chris had locked him out of that whole part of his life in response to his latest mistake. That Chris was somehow finding the time in the few hours they weren't together each day to murder and hide a woman. It made no logical sense, but that had never been an inhibitor to fear, so he gradually became more and more clingy, following Chris around even when he had no reason to, or when it impeded his own plans for the day. So it was that he ended up loitering while Chris was going through the usual motions of chatting about his sexual exploits, minus their lethal endings, with their slightly older and more settled workmates who liked to live through him vicariously. This time when pressed for details of his latest "rags," Chris came out with something completely unexpected. He suggested that he was thinking of finding a nice girl and settling down.

James nearly collapsed. He had never planned for the future because all of his past experience had taught him how quickly plans fall apart, but he was emotionally invested in his relationship with Chris, even if the other man had special needs that he wasn't capable of fulfilling, and he had assumed that they were going to go on with their lives in at least a similar way in the future. The idea of Chris leaving him and settling down into some nice normal straight relationship was an even worse nightmare than the idea of Chris murdering women for pleasure. James' sexuality wasn't exactly a secret among his workmates, and if it weren't for Chris's quick wit and protection, the jibes about it may very well have escalated into something more vicious, but even so, he couldn't say anything to Chris about this terrible idea in front of his workmates without appearing like the jealous love-struck homosexual that most of them had already pegged him as. As Chris joked with the men about whether they had any sisters or daughters that they could hook him up with, James' whole world shattered around him.

Vicki Howell

In the days after the death of Sylvia Pitman, Worrell's attitude towards Miller remained frosty, and James remained confused about the meaning of everything that his beloved was putting him through. Chris continued to talk about finding himself a more permanent girl. One who wouldn't vanish after one use. Although he didn't use those exact terms when trying to entice their mutual friends into setting him up with their friends, daughters, and sisters. The distance between the two men remained despite James' efforts the night before to be supportive. Everything was becoming hazy to the traumatised Miller. The meaning of things that he thought before were as solid as the earth beneath him was starting to waiver. He had always believed that killing was wrong. That violence was wrong. But the people who had taught him that had also tried to teach him that love, the kind of love that he felt towards other men, was an abomination. Why did one hold true and the other one fall apart?

While Chris went to the post office, James parked the car with growled orders to meet up at Victoria Square afterwards. He sat alone in the car for a few minutes, his thoughts buzzing and his panic growing. What was he going to do if Chris left him? If he really left him and settled down with some woman and bought a house and had a normal life? Chris might have been a monster on the inside, but to all appearances, he would have been quite a catch. What would it mean if Chris left him? Would he even trust James to keep quiet after they parted ways, or would he kill him, too? James shuddered at the thought of being like one of Chris' girls, pinned down under the muscular planes of his body. He shifted uncomfortably in his seat and glanced around guiltily. There were worse ways to go. He wasn't volunteering just yet, but if he had to die he would at least die happy knowing that he was giving Chris the kind of pleasure that he deserved. James wasn't a religious man, and if you had asked him to be a martyr to some god up in the sky he probably would have laughed in your face, but for this, he would make that ultimate sacrifice. Now that he could see how close he was to losing Chris forever, death seemed like a small price to pay if it meant that he could spend his final moments looking into his beloved's eyes.

He started trying to do something entirely unfamiliar, sitting there in those snatched moments that he was away from

Chris. He tried to come up with a solution to his problems instead of just letting them wash over him. He wasn't as charming as Chris, and he would never have the younger man's way with words and women, but he could try to pick up a girl. He could try to pick up a girl and offer her up to Chris. To show that he was willing, even if he wasn't exactly comfortable. It was an extreme solution, but just hinting to Chris that they should go out looking for a girl didn't seem like it was enough. Being a passive observer didn't seem to be enough to make up for what he had done in spoiling Chris' time with Julie. He needed to do more to win back his friend's trust. He wanted to do more than just watch. He sat back in his seat with a shiver. He wanted to do more than just watch. He wanted Chris to make him a part of it, the same way that he had made him a part of every other part of his life. He wanted all of Chris. He wanted the bright smiles and the black moods. James wanted the infectious laugh and the heat that radiated off of Chris when he spoke about his victims. The price didn't matter.

James got out of the car and stalked off in search of Chris, eyeing all the young pretty girls on the street as he went. He had never really looked at them before, so he didn't know how to judge which ones might be interested. With men it was a whole different dance, less about attraction and more about safety as you tried to get one another to admit to being interested in men at all. He smiled at a few, and of those few most scowled back at him. He supposed that on his own he was a pretty unappealing proposition, particularly to the young girls who Chris preferred. Somebody like Chris was what they imagined when they were thinking of taking an older man as a lover. James suspected he looked less like a fantasy and more like a horror story waiting to happen. He glanced down at his hands, calloused and weather beaten, and realised with a start just how old he probably seemed to all these pretty young things. When he was with Chris his age didn't seem to matter even if he had more than a decade on everyone around him, but nothing seemed to matter when he was with Chris. Still, it was going to be a problem. He couldn't exactly use Chris as a prop to pick up a new girl as a surprise for Chris.

When he came into Victoria Square, he ground to a halt with a startled little laugh. Chris had found a girl all by himself. His face had lit up like it always did when he was charming women, but even when he met James' gaze over her head the smile didn't fade. James didn't know what to do. He smiled back, but that didn't seem enough. Just a few days ago this would have been the start of another nightmare for him, but now it was like Chris had read his mind. He gave Chris a nod and that seemed to be enough to convince him that James was on board. The full power of his smile was turned back on the unsuspecting girl.

When James got closer, he was almost startled by the girl's appearance. He wasn't the only one looking older than expected that day. While Chris's usual girls were barely teenagers, this woman must have been older than Chris. James wondered if this had something to do with all of that settling down talk. If it had all stemmed from Chris just being in the mood for someone a little bit older for a change. If Chris was picking his dates under the delusion that they might actually lead to a relationship, then this was a sensible choice. He couldn't settle down with any of the teenagers who he usually chased after—many of them were still in school. It was just as possible that Chris had picked her as an easier mark, an older woman who might be flattered by the attention of a younger man without any of the predatory overtones that he usually had to navigate around in his pursuit of teens. Chris wouldn't talk about the details afterwards. He seemed to prefer pretending that his little liaisons didn't happen at all, even before he started killing the girls. He would brag about girls in abstract terms to his buddies at work, but with James he never shared a single thought about them.

When Chris introduced him, James went the extra mile, layering on all of the charm that he could muster, smiling at the woman as she prattled on about herself. As if any of it mattered. Still, James knew that the easiest way to get caught in a lie was to forget details, so he dutifully smiled and nodded along as Vicki talked about her work as a nurse's aide. He asked questions to keep the conversation going. He laughed at her jokes. He played up his effete mannerisms and set the woman completely at ease. Chris kept looking at James whenever she wasn't paying attention, bemused and confused in equal measure by James's newfound attentive streak. His expression slowly turned into a smirk as James invited the girl out for a drive in the Adelaide Hills. With not one but two charming men inviting her for a drive on a lovely day, it was almost inevitable that Vicki would say yes.

James drove, with Chris in his usual spot on the passenger's side, but while they had repeated this pattern dozens of times, James seemed different this time. He laughed along with the girl as Chris cracked jokes. He caught her gaze in the rearview mirror and flashed her a smile. For the very first time he did everything that he could to make the whole experience as smooth as possible, and he could tell from the way that Chris responded with renewed enthusiasm and energy that it was appreciated. When they arrived in the middle of nowhere, the sun was still far from setting. Chris slipped into the back seat beside Vicki and she started to respond to his amorous advances before James even had the chance to mutter something about going for a walk. He very carefully left his pack of cigarettes in the car and then walked away to let Chris get down to business as usual.

A few minutes later, he crept back to the car, careful not to make any sound. In the backseat he could see Chris, but Vicki, laying on the back seats, was out of sight. Chris had undone the buttons of his shirt, and the pale expanse of his chest bobbed up into view as he looked up and met James' wide-mouthed gasp with a wink. He dipped back out of sight and, taking it as an invitation, James crept closer. Vicki was still wearing most of her clothes, but she was so lost in lust that she barely seemed to notice Chris looping the rope around her wrists as they kissed. Chris was smiling as he kissed her, going through the mechanical motions while keeping his concentration firmly on his knots.

James didn't know how long he stood there watching and dreaming that Chris's strong hand were tightening the ropes around his wrists like that, that Chris's lips were moving against his own. Chris glanced up at him again and laughed out loud, muffled only a little by the car's windows. If Vicki was startled to notice James standing outside the car, she didn't show it. Chris leant over her to roll down the window, then he threw James' cigarettes at him, still laughing. "Get out of here you old peeping tom!"

James bent to pick up his cigarettes and gave Vicki a mumbled apology. Just as he was starting to back away, temptation took over and he looked back into the car. Chris met his gaze and licked his lips. It was hard to tell if Chris was doing it just to mess with him or as some sort of taunt, but for James it was like looking into the face of God, a perfect moment of clarity. He loved that man so much it felt like a hook in his chest dragging him forward. Chris descended back onto Vicki and James managed to tear himself away with a cigarette pinched between his dry lips.

Normally, the walk was fraught with tension and fear—he was waiting for some tell-tale sound or warning that Chris was unleashing his darker impulses—but tonight it was a relief. He might have wanted to show Chris that he was invested in their lives together but actually watching Chris screwing someone else might have been too much to bear. He wasn't sure if his stomach could have handled watching a woman being choked to death either, although if he were honest it troubled him a lot less than the idea of Chris sleeping with other people. He wondered if that made him a bad person, and if spending every waking moment with a murderer made him more accepting of things that you shouldn't accept, but that introspection passed quickly in the flood of memories. Chris smiling at him. Chris's shirt unbuttoned. Chris licking his lips. Those moments meant more than the worries. He had lived his whole life waiting for the future to come along and ruin everything. The only difference was that now he had a reason to care about the present. Chris was acting strangely tonight, probably still angry about the last time, but James was sure that he could win him back now that he knew what to do. It was the same thing that he had always done, submitting to Chris absolutely in all things.

James didn't hate Vicki. Any jealousy that he used to feel was melting away in his new wave of acceptance. If anything, he was grateful to the girl for helping Chris get what he really wanted. Of all the people that Chris had met in his life, James was probably the first one to really understand his needs, to really know him for who he truly was. That was an intimacy that these stupid girls would only get to know for an instant in the midst of the rush of pure panic as they struggled for air. James' bond with him ran deeper than these girls could even dream of. He was Chris's best friend, he was the keeper of all his darkest secrets, and most importantly, he loved him despite everything that he knew. He loved him through all the dark moods and the outbursts. He loved him in prison and in freedom. He loved Chris so much that he could willingly sacrifice the things that he wanted so that Chris could get what he needed. Wasn't that the real meaning of love? He didn't hate Vicki any more than he hated the sandwich that Chris ate for lunch, she was just some little morsel that Chris could devour to satisfy his body. She wasn't special. She wasn't even the kind of sandwich that Chris really liked to eat. The man was just hungry. Any girl from anywhere would have done, this one just happened to be the one who fell into his lap. Chris chose James. He chose him to spend his life with. Not these girls who he discarded after he had used them up. What did James care about what happened to them? They were the ones flinging themselves at a stranger, slithering into the backseat with him after only a few minutes of conversation. They were bringing it on themselves. They were the ones who were choosing to die. If they really wanted to live they would take better care of themselves. They wouldn't come out into the middle of nowhere with a murderer and his accomplice.

Miller kept his walk quite short that night. Until now he had been scared to walk in on James during the act, but tonight it would be his proving. He could walk right up to the car, see Chris killing, and do nothing but smile. He knew he could force a smile onto his face even if he didn't feel like it—that was half of lying after all—but tonight with all of these wild thoughts running through his head, with all the spite and jealousy he had felt toward all of the whores who had come before finally finding an outlet, he knew that he would be smiling for real.

When he got back to the car, Chris was leaning on the bumper, still as a statue and smoking as usual. His shoulders were drawn up and the scowl on his face was already firmly etched. Vicki was nowhere to be seen, also as usual. James smiled at him, but Chris wasn't focusing—he was staring right through him. His glazed eyes were doing nothing more than tracking motion like some mindless animal. The growl just added to the impression that Chris was something less than human. It started deep in his chest and the rolled up and out of him when James opened his mouth to speak. He started cursing and roaring at James before he could get a word in. He unleashed a torrent of abuse on James, insulting his intelligence, his sexual preferences, his personal grooming, and everything else that he could think of. He came up off of the car with his fists clenched, advancing on James and spitting vitriol. He didn't hear James. He wasn't listening. He just screamed and screamed and couldn't seem to understand why the other man, the weaker man, wasn't withering. That was how it was meant to go. This was the script that they were used to following. James was meant to come back and find the girl dead. Then James was meant to try to convince him that killing was wrong, and Chris would crush him emotionally until he accepted it. Over and over. That was part of the ritual that made this whole exercise so entertaining. Chris couldn't understand why James had to spoil even that. His fury grew with every step that he drew closer to James. With every insult that failed to make the weaker man crumble he got louder and louder. He was close enough to hit James by the time he fell silent. Close enough to lean forward and kiss if James just had the courage.

The knife was in its usual place, sheathed on his belt at the small of his back. Even if the top few buttons of his shirt were left undone and it was hanging untucked, there was no chance that he would forget to put the knife back where it belonged. James knew how dangerous Chris was, both from their nights out here where he murdered girls for fun and from the few times when they were back in prison that things had gotten physical, and he understood very clearly that despite all of the love Chris obviously felt for him, it was entirely possible that the man he loved might kill him if he didn't handle him right. He had been easing Chris out of his black moods for a long time now. He no longer felt the insults or the fear of violence the way that he supposed he should. When all that mattered was Chris, worrying about himself seemed like a waste of time. Eventually, Chris ran out of breath, and he heard what James was saying back to him.

"It's all right. Don't worry about it. It's fine. We're fine."

Chris stared at James as if he had grown an extra head. "She is in the back seat, under the blanket. I killed her. You get that, right?"

James smiled at him, a little wryly, and nodded. "So, we need to get rid of the body, right? Just like before. It is no problem, man."

The anger drained out of Chris almost instantly and he fell silent. James could almost hear his big beautiful brain whirring to make sense of this new information, to change up the ritual to accommodate this new variable. They quietly climbed back into the car and James started it up. He glanced back at the lumpy blanket in the back seat and sighed wistfully. He might be on Chris's side, and it might have been all her fault, but that didn't mean he wasn't sorry that somebody had been killed. Chris seemed to read his mind.

Softly, almost morosely, he said, "She seemed such a nice lady."

James shrugged. "Oh well. Plenty more fish in the sea."

Then he pulled the car back onto the dirt track road and sped off through the early evening glow towards their special place, out by Truro.

Connie Iordanides

The time that passed between each of the girls was getting shorter. Despite the strange fluctuations in the relationship between James and Chris, whatever force was driving the younger man only seemed to grow more and more intense. He needed to go out hunting sooner and sooner after each kill. Neither man acknowledged it any more than Chris was willing to acknowledge the latest change that James had just inflicted on him, but James had learned to adapt to Chris's moods long ago—to predict which way the wind was blowing and to move things around so that Chris could get his way with the minimum amount of friction. So, when they started to drive around Adelaide looking for a new girl just a day after they had dumped Vicki under a pile of sticks out by Truro, it came as no surprise. Chris was his usual calm self as they trawled around the streets of Adelaide. They rolled by the train station, the bus station, and bars that usually served up hot and cold running women, but for some reason none of them were taking Chris's fancy. For a moment, James felt a flutter in his stomach. The last one had been an older woman. Maybe this time Chris would go even further afield in his experimentation and pick out something that James might enjoy looking at, too. It wasn't like he hadn't shown some inclinations in that direction. The jealousy would be worse if Chris picked a man, he was certain of that, but the relief when it was over and Chris enacted his revenge for him would be even sweeter. When Chris gave an excitable yelp and patted his arm, James had no idea what to expect until he finally caught sight of the two girls coming out of the cinema. They were exactly Chris's type. Neither could have been a year out of high school if they were that. Chris had never tried to bag two girls at once before, although James had spotted that particular configuration of leather-clad bodies showing up in his magazines often enough. It would present a unique challenge. James let out a silent prayer that Chris wasn't going to ask him to fake his way through a double date so that he could get them into the car. James sincerely doubted that he could pull it off, and then Chris's fury would have been terrible to behold. James knew that Chris didn't like to talk about his plans ahead of time, that he liked to watch him squirm and adapt to please him, but he was almost ready to ask what their play was going to be when his prayer was answered. One of the girls peeled off to head for the bus stop with a wave back to her friend.

James pulled up by the roadside, and Chris began to lay on the charm before the window was even rolled partway down. "Hey there, what did you see?"

The girl was young enough that this kind of direct attention was a novelty to her, so where an older and wiser woman would have known to demure and pull away from a conversation with a strange man that didn't seem to have a point, Connie answered right back without thinking with the title of the film. Chris's face cracked into a cherubic grin. "Me and Jim were just talking about going to see that one next week. Was it any good?"

James accepted that his name was going to be Jim for the rest of the evening—that was hardly difficult to handle at all. In all of his time with Chris, he couldn't recall a single time that they had gone out to see a movie, but it was a pretty universal experience, so there wasn't much of a lie to get caught out in there either. The specific movie was a bit trickier. He started scanning the posters around the cinema entrance to find the title she had mumbled, hunting for any detail that he could use to support the latest deep dive into a deception that Chris had plunged them into without warning or a moment's thought.

Chris had charisma on his side that would be enough to carry him through. James had to use his brain. Chris was a natural born liar. James had to work for every line that these girls swallowed. Connie was anxiously warbling through the merits of the film as if anyone gave a damn about her opinion on anything, but when there was a brief lull in her film review, James snuck in the tiny bit of knowledge that he had been able to scrape from the posters, along with his usual disarming comment hinting at how harmless he was. He double-checked the name of the leading man with her then gave her a salacious wink saying, "He's a dreamboat though, isn't he."

He saw Connie's eyes flick from his face to Chris and back, her understanding of the situation warping further and further from the lethal truth. Chris didn't like to play gay, and he was too predatory in his advances for the deception to last long anyway, but like all great salesmen and psychopaths, he lived in the moment. He would ad-lib along with any lie in that moment if it would get the girl into the car. If he switched the script afterwards she would put it down to a misunderstanding. Particularly about something so potentially sensitive.

A car ground to a halt behind them, tooting its horn at them for blocking the road, and it was all the prompting that Chris needed. "Oh shoot, we weren't done talking. Thanks for the advice little miss. I don't suppose we can offer you a lift as thanks?"

Connie stood frozen and wide-eyed. Stranger danger campaigns in Australia wouldn't kick in for another decade or more, so all that was protecting her in that moment was her own sense of social awkwardness and whatever instincts for self-preservation that were screaming at her from deep in her animal brain. When the car behind them tooted its horn again, she caved. Chris hopped out and she slid into the front seat alongside the two men, obviously uncomfortable but not uncomfortable enough to try to scramble over one of their laps to escape. James pulled away from the kerb with a wave to the car behind. Connie finally introduced herself by name, but Chris's usual charm seemed to be faltering in the face of her nerves, and there was only so much that James could do to seem harmless. She asked them to take her home, giving James her parents' address, which he nodded along to dutifully as if he was actually listening and actually going to take her there. She was twitchy. Every time that Chris shifted around in his seat to talk to her she would jerk away. Every time James said something from behind her, her head would twist around so fast that he was concerned that she was going to hurt herself, so before long James just shut up and let Chris try to coax her back from whatever anxiety had enveloped her. When she caught a glimpse of a road sign for Wingfield, her panic escalated into screaming. They were taking her in the opposite direction to home. They were taking her.

Chris, never one to tolerate much noise, clamped a hand over the girl's mouth as they drove, but as she struggled and clawed at him his temper flared. He pushed Connie through into the backseat as James tried to keep the car going straight and then climbed through after her. She squealed as his hands began to rove over her, and when he drew the rope out from his pocket she began to wail so loudly that he had to hit her before she drew attention. While she was momentarily stunned, he got her hands bound in a loop of rope before clamping his hands back around her mouth and bearing her down onto the floor in the back. This was a level of recklessness that neither man had ever attempted before. James was trying to ignore what was happening behind him for his own safety as much as anything else. Every time he looked into the rearview mirror he became fixated and the car began to swerve. He forced himself to keep his eyes on the road and to ignore first the muffled screams, then the sound of tearing cotton. James wet his lips and kept his eyes locked straight along the headlight beams, letting his ears absorb every sound like a tease. That sounded almost like a slap. That low growl was Chris, horny or angry or both. That yelp, suddenly cut off, was the sound of Chris' big strong hands closing around her throat. The distinct sound of his trouser zip sliding down was like a low rumble, perfectly in tune with the soft roar of the engine as they tore through the streets and out into the wilds.

Out on the edge of Wingfield, James pulled the car to a screeching halt by the side of the road, throwing up a cloud of dust. He slammed on the handbrake and spun around to watch as the engine shuddered to a halt. As an afterthought,

James flicked off the headlights, hiding them just that little bit more from any unwanted attention. Even without any lights on, there was still enough sunshine streaming over the horizon to light up the scene in the backseat in beautiful hues of red.

Connie was half on the back seats and half on the floor. Her tied hands were pushed up above her head and she seemed to have forgotten they were there. Her clothes were almost entirely intact. It wasn't about the bodies for Chris. It was about the actions. He was still fully clothed, too, except for his undone trousers slowly slipping down the curve of his backside with each movement. He was pressed between her legs, using his weight to keep her pinned in place as he toyed with her. Her face was bright red and her eyes were bulging and rolling around like a horse's when it goes wild. Whatever rational mind that she had under those pretty curls was gone and nothing but fear remained. She strained away from Chris even though there was nowhere for her to go. As if leaning a little to the left would make her any less his. As if there were any way to get away from what he was doing to her. Or what he was going to do to her next. James' eyes slid right past her. She didn't matter in the grand scheme of things—she was just a means to an end. He looked at Chris. There was a light in his eyes that James had only ever seen a glimmer of during their time together. When Chris had forced him down onto his knees with barely any effort. When Chris was deep in his blackest moods and James had to drag him away from civilisation before he did something so bad there would be no coming back from jail if someone saw it. Those two things were linked; they were two paths to the same place within the tangled thicket of Chris's mind. His mouth hung open, and James could see the tip of his tongue playing over the edge of his teeth. The muscles in his arms corded beneath his shirt as he held the girl pinioned in place by her throat and the press of his hips. His movements were slow, almost languid, like he had all night to get to where he was going and he was going to enjoy the ride. It was almost completely the opposite of Chris's approach to everything else in life. At work, at a bar, everything was smash and grab and satisfaction as soon as he could reach it, but here and now he slowed to a crawl. All of those times that he had James pleasure him with his mouth it had taken until he was lock-jawed, choking and aching before Chris was done. James had always thought it was because he was a man, because Chris wasn't enjoying himself properly. Now he realised that it was just Chris's way.

The other man was lost in the moment, completely oblivious to James staring at him. Passion seeped out of every pore as the sweat started to run down his chest. He wasn't choking her to death, just to the point of blacking out, then he would pull back and let her recover enough to realise what was happening to her before he tightened his grip again. He did it over and over, flexing with each thrust, tendons standing out from his wrists as he choked her. There was a rhythm hidden in his movements, a steady beat, maybe the rhythm of his heart. James found his hand slipping down to press against the front of his jeans as he watched. This was what he had been waiting for. This was what he had worked for. This perfect moment with Chris, just the two of them and some tool that they could toss out into the desert when they were done with her. He hissed out a soft breath as he touched himself, so quiet he was certain that Chris couldn't hear him, but something about his body language or the motion caught Chris' attention. He turned the full weight of his predatory gaze on James and the other man crumbled, hand slipping away to rest by his side. Chris growled, "Isn't it time for your walk?"

James found himself breathless as he shook his head. He was dry mouthed when he tried to speak. "I... I am fine where I am."

Chris blinked at him. He flexed his hands around the girl's throat as a low keening wail started to escape her lips. "Get out of the car."

"I can stay. I can watch. It is all right. You don't have to—you don't have to hide anything from me Chris," James could hear pleading starting to seep into his voice, but Chris was having none of it.

"Get out of the bloody car and don't forget your bloody cigarettes this time."

James did as he was told. Whatever Chris needed, apparently it wasn't to have him hanging around and watching as he did his thing. Maybe it was embarrassing for him, like masturbating, since the girls weren't people. Maybe this was a good thing. Maybe he wanted James out of the car because he recognised him as a friend and an equal, someone who he wouldn't want to watch him doing what he had to do to get off. James never lied to anyone as much as he lied to himself. He may have been constantly adapting to suit Chris's needs, but Chris was constantly changing, too. Every time that he killed, he refined his ritual, but more than that—he changed his plans to counter whatever steps James had taken to please him. Whatever it took to keep the man in a constant state of torment. James would never see it that way, understanding each failure as nothing more than his own inability to understand Chris's needs rather than a deliberate moving of the goalposts. He walked a little along the road and lit up one of the cigarettes Chris insisted that he bring along. His hands were shaking, but it wasn't all fear, even if some of it was. He was excited. More excited than he had been since the last time Chris had let him please him. He had come so close to being a part of Chris's pleasure. He was shivering with anticipation at what the next girl would bring. He was getting closer now. He could feel it. Any day now he was going to slip right inside that storm of emotion around Chris and become part of his passion plays. He was going to be with Chris, the way that he was meant to be with Chris.

After the cigarette was done, he stood in the slowly cooling air for only a few minutes before the car door slammed. He jogged back to find Chris lighting up. The men nodded to each other in companionable silence. There was a blanket spread over the mess in the backseat that neither of them commented on. James came to stand beside Chris, which he had learned was easier than looking at him without staring. After a moment Chris said, "You did all right tonight. You know that?"

James smiled, "Yeah?"

"Not bad. Not great but not bad. Don't make it weird again." Chris might have been smiling around his cigarette, but in the dull orange glow it could have been a trick of the shadows.

James scuffed at the dirt with his toe. "I'll do better next time. I promise."

Chris punched him in the shoulder. "Making it weird again mate. Just—do what I need, yeah? And don't get so involved. It's not about you. You know?"

"I know mate. Sorry. Wasn't trying to spoil anyone's fun. Didn't understand what you wanted before but I think I do now." James kept his eyes off Chris. If he stayed careful he could do this. If he didn't get carried away.

"Don't worry about it. Let's take a drive, yeah?"

They climbed back into the car and headed off for their usual stretch of scrubland in Truro. They tossed Connie in a heap, and while Chris lay back on the warm hood and looked up at the stars, James carefully gathered enough sticks to cover her. A little ritual of his own that didn't go unnoticed, even if Chris chose not to comment. James was getting too comfortable. He was starting to enjoy all of this instead of hating it. It wasn't giving Chris the kick he needed anymore. If James had just gone on being horrified, then tonight's performance in the car, making him watch, would have been perfect. Instead, he was going to have to come up with some new way to torture his old follower. When the job was done, Chris laid a hand on James' sleeve and gave him a little reward. They drove to the racetracks and parked outside, spending the rest of the night drifting in and out of a shallow sleep in the car, their hands almost touching on the middle of the bench in the front seat.

Deborah Lamb

Chris's new torments came fast and hard. The first of them came the very next day when he was politely introduced to Chris's new steady girlfriend, who was currently going by Amelia. After the death of the older nurse, James thought that Chris had shaken off the notion of settling down, that their evenings spent trawling for fresh rags, fresh prey, were a clear indicator that Chris had abandoned the idea entirely in favour of their usual life together. He had grossly underestimated Chris's ability to multitask. After James had stopped following him around like a lost puppy, he had been free to start chasing up the vague hints that they had picked up from the network of lowlifes and criminals on women who might be interested in him. Both men crossed paths with other people that they had been in prison with frequently, even if they didn't actively seek out a social life with Adelaide's criminal element, and through them and the limited reach of their work buddies it hadn't taken long to get the young, attractive, and employed Worrell a girlfriend.

James and Chris wandered into one of their usual dive bars early on after work. They had been working on a street only a few minutes walk away. With their drinks in hand, they weaved their way to one of the booths by the jukebox, and it was only after Chris had slung himself in that James eyes adjusted enough to the dim light to realise that there was already someone in the booth. He quickly plastered on his usual fake smile and met a fairly genuine one coming right back. She wasn't a teenager, but she wasn't as old as the nurse had been either. She wasn't exactly Chris's type, but if any of the girls that Chris pursued had lived long enough to grow up, they might have ended up looking like Amelia. They spent the whole evening in the bar chatting and drinking, and to James' absolute horror, he slowly came to realise that he liked the woman. That he could see himself being friends with her. The shape of his future with Chris started to reshape itself again. He was going to end up as the weird uncle who came around for dinner every week and told off-color jokes then went home alone to an empty apartment and a hollow life. He was going to be the one who took dad out drinking and dropped him off in the early hours of the morning smelling of sweat and other women. He didn't want to hurt Amelia. He hadn't really wanted to hurt anyone, but the girls, they just kept throwing themselves at Chris. At the end of the night, he dropped Amelia and Chris off at her apartment, and the years opened up like a gaping void ahead of him. Decades of dropping Chris off at home. A lifetime of knowing that he had lost him but still never having the guts to completely let go. It was going to be hell, but what was he meant to do, deny Chris what he wanted? The next day, Chris chatted with him as usual, and when James brought up the subject of his girlfriend it was treated as just another normal part of the conversation. Even when they were alone, Chris rarely let his guard down for long. It was no surprise that he couldn't bring himself to share the true meaning behind his new romantic endeavour. The men on the crew had all seemed highly amused that Chris was going steady with a girl after all the time they had known him, and one or two cast a meaningful look in James' direction to see just how badly he was taking the news. His fake smile remained plastered in place at all times. He had been using it daily since Chris started murdering girls. He never suspected that he would need to use it because Chris was dating. At the end of the day when they piled into the car, James was expecting to end up parked in a booth watching Chris and Amelia making eyes at each other again all night. A wave of relief rolled over him when he realised that they were going out looking for girls to murder instead. It was a Saturday night and the crowds were thick, but there were very few women out on their own. Enough girls had gone missing in the last few weeks that it was starting to draw attention. They stopped for drinks in a few different bars and rolled past their usual haunts, but it was after midnight before the crowds started to thin and they could pick out girls by themselves wandering the streets, looking for trouble. They rolled along towards the neon lights of the City Bowl, past the garish colours and electronic chatter of the pinball arcades that lined the promenade. They didn't have to go looking for Deborah Lamb. She came looking for them, flagging down the car as they passed with the customary jerk of the thumb and flash of her leg from under her short skirt.

"Hi fellas, you going my way?"

Chris rarely got to play the role of the pursued instead of the pursuer lately, so he seemed to delight in the girl's forward approach. "Depends where you are heading, I guess."

They negotiated back and forth as James chuckled along. Chris seemed to like her, even if she was a little on the old side for him, and he had already wrangled enough information out of her to be sure that she wasn't going to be missed by anybody. Not tonight and probably not ever. Hitchhikers had always been a personal favourite for Chris—victims who came gift-wrapped and handed to him with a reason to get in the car. She slid into the backseat almost before Chris had finished offering her a ride up to Port Gawler.

When they got there, things went smoother and quicker than usual. It was a beautiful night and there was nobody around, so James drove them right down onto the beach and parked. The sand was still clinging to the last of the day's warmth, and even the breeze coming in off the sea wasn't enough to fight against the perpetual warmth of Adelaide. Deborah knew the kind of fare that a hitchhiker usually had to pay. She was shimmying her underwear down over her stockings as she got out of the car, and she looked from one man to the other with a wry grin. Chris grinned right back and James loudly announced that he was going to take a walk since it was such a nice night. When he walked away, the two of them were already giggling and tumbling on the sand. He didn't expect that would last long.

He knew that Chris didn't want him watching, so he really took his time on this walk, trying to use the time alone to think everything through. Maybe this was for the best. Chris settling down. Maybe it would be enough to calm him down and make him stop all of this. James had a pretty low opinion of the police in Adelaide, but even he would admit that eventually they were going to catch on if Chris kept up the pace of killing four girls a week. He could still remember the time before Chris started killing, or at least before he knew about Chris's murderous impulses. It wouldn't be so terrible to go back to that. To lower the intensity a little. If he wasn't going to be able to have the intimacy he wanted with Chris, then settling in for something more sustainable sounded like a far better plan than their current trajectory. Chris lived in the moment, whether by choice or because of whatever defect in his brain made him think murdering girls was a good hobby, but James had always been looking to their future. If he had to settle for a quieter future that could stretch on for years instead of the blaze of glory that they had been on course to go out in, he would take whatever was on offer. Whatever scraps of Chris fell from the table he would take, like the obedient, attention-starved dog that he was.

When he got back to the car, there was no sign of Deborah Lamb, but Chris was busy around the far side. As James arrived, he saw Chris pushing the last of a mound of sand with his foot until it trickled down into the shallow indentation where Deborah's body lay. It could only have been a few minutes ago that Chris finished with her, so Miller blessed his luck. He would not have felt so lucky if he realised that beneath the sand, Deborah Lamb was still alive, gasping for air and filling her lungs with the sand that Worrell had just dumped on top of her bound body. Chris was smiling and joking when he arrived, shutting him out of this dark part of his life in stages now that he had recognised that James might have taken some joy in it. The confusion that flitted back and forth in the old man's eyes had made the change of tactics all worthwhile.

The Final Victim

For the next week, James and Chris had the social life of normal people instead of deranged killers. They went out for a drink after work. They lived together in their apartment. Chris went out on dates with his new girlfriend while James sat home alone. They even went visiting old friends on occasion, which is how they came upon Deborah Skuse sitting on the floor of an empty apartment crying.

Skuse had been dating one of the men's old friends from prison who had either had to move on quickly due to his less-than-legal business interests or, as she seemed to believe, because he was too much of a coward to break up with her face to face. He had left their shared apartment while she was at work and taken all of their belongings and furnishings with him. Despite his obvious shortcomings, it had left Deborah devastated, and while Chris didn't have any instinct for empathy, James had enough for both of them. He sat and held Deborah's hand as she cried and nodded along as she rambled furiously. In the end, Chris' patience started to wear thin, so he proposed a solution. They would take a trip up to Mount Gambier for the weekend, have a few drinks, have a few laughs and start making some new, happy memories. Even though Chris had no vested interest in the conversation beyond making it end as quickly as possible, he quickly charmed the vulnerable Skuse and convinced her that some time away from the city was exactly what she needed.

When Friday night rolled around, James had packed a bag and was ready to go, but Chris was ready to just go to his bed after a long day's work. He had to be convinced, very delicately, to go through with the plans that he had invented for their weekend. He wasn't happy about the prospect of being stuck out in the middle of nowhere with nothing to do, but with a little coaxing and the reminder that they could buy liquor to take up with them, he became a little more pliant. He could get drunk just as well up in the hills as in some bar, and if the urge took him while he was away, Deborah had already proven herself pretty susceptible to his charms. As for James, he thought that a little time away from everything might help to clear his head. Ever since he met Chris, his whole life had revolved around him. Ever since Chris got out of prison, things had been in a constant state of outright chaos. James needed to take some time to work out what he was going to do when things started to slow down.

The first night went smoothly enough. Chris spent the night flirting with Deborah until James was convinced that he was going to have to go and take a walk for an hour. He managed to catch Chris alone and obliquely referenced the fact that people knew that Deborah was coming out to the mountain with them. It was close enough to talking about the murderous activities that were a permanently taboo topic that Chris immediately fell into sullen silence and stayed there until they shuffled off to their respective beds shortly afterwards. The next day, Chris was up and drinking before the other two even stirred. He continued to sulk and scowl throughout the morning until they all were forced to admit that this trip had been a bad idea. Chris's black mood showed no signs of lifting even when they announced their plan to return home. He wouldn't speak to James at all, banishing him to the back seat of the car and taking the driver's position for himself. He had Deborah sit in the front beside him, mainly to hold his beer as he drove.

He tore down the mountain road as fast as the car could go. Within moments, Deborah was wheedling him to slow down, but he paid no attention, barely even acknowledging her constant stream of mumblings except when she pulled the beer bottle out of reach. Then he leant over with a sneer and snatched it from her. James groaned in the back seat. This was worse than he had imagined one of Chris's black moods could be, and he was already so angry at James that any attempt to soothe him was just going to rile him up further. James put his face in his hands and hoped that Chris would calm down before they got back into the city limits. The police would pull them over if they were going this speed, and if they stopped Chris, then he was going to lash out. Things didn't go well for ex-convicts lashing out at the police. He would be lucky to walk away with less than a decade on his sentence. He would come out a withered old man like James. Chris growled, "I've got a headache, you stupid bitch. Shut up."

Deborah barely seemed to hear him, eyes on the road rapidly vanishing in front of her. She was shaking and begging him in a shrill voice, "Please, slow down. Just slow down. I don't want to die."

Chris snarled, "You think I'm stupid? You think I don't know how to drive? Just shut up, will you?"

She screamed, "Slow down! You're going to crash."

What came out of Chris was less of a shout and more of a roar. "Will you shut your damned mouth! I am trying to drive here!"

That was when they tire blew out.

James didn't remember anything afterwards. The events had to be pieced together by the police from the mess that was left behind. The rubber smeared on the asphalt. The scatter of the debris. The placement of the wreckage. Chris tried to keep control of the car when the front tire blew out, but he was going too fast and the back end began to fishtail as he slammed on the brakes. The car careered out of control and began to slip and slide across the lane into the oncoming traffic. With a truck heading straight for him, Worrell jerked desperately on the wheel and sent the car off the side of the road. It flipped. Rolling twice down the embankment and out onto the grass, flinging the passengers out of the open windows as it rolled. Traffic slammed to a halt up on the road and bystanders came rushing down to help, but there was little that they could do. An ambulance was called from an emergency phone along the road, but it was only coming for Miller. Both Chris Worrell and Deborah Skuse were dead on the scene. The final victims of Chris's terrible black moods.

For several weeks, James Miller recovered slowly from his injuries in the hospital, but he didn't seem to care one way or the other if he survived or not. He would answer any question asked of him, but otherwise he was completely shut down. Chris was dead so nothing else mattered. His family tried to coax him into speaking, but he had just lost the will to try. Once his broken shoulder had set enough that he was allowed out of bed and they were certain that his concussion wasn't going to kill him, he signed himself out of the hospital so that he could attend Chris's funeral. It was a quiet and sombre affair attended by his workmates from the crew and a few ex-convicts who he hadn't managed to alienate yet. James would have spent his last cent making it into a big event if he had been capable, but as it was the work crew managed to put on a little buffet dinner at one of their homes afterwards. It was there that James crossed paths with Amelia again for the first time since Chris's death. He bumped into her in his coworker's back garden where a barbeque had been set up to prepare food for the gathering. She had been crying but seemed relatively composed. Of all the people in the world, she was the only one left who James felt any kinship towards, so he felt obliged to offer her any comfort that he could. Even if it was in his own terrible and clumsy way.

"Did they tell you the results from Chris's autopsy?"

She didn't recognise him for a moment when he came lumbering over to her, bruises still yellowing half of his face, and it took her a moment to recognise that this wasn't some friend of a friend showing inappropriate and prurient interest. She shook her head. James pressed on. "I think that he had a brain clot. A blood clot in his brain, I mean. I've been trying to get him to talk to someone for months. He has these moods. He—he had these moods when he was so angry. He just got so angry about nothing and you had to get him away from people, you know? He wasn't right."

She shook her head slowly. Chris had been careful to hide his black moods from everyone whom he expected to live. Blending in was a valuable survival technique for monsters in human skin. Her non-compliance didn't seem to register for

James. He had been locked in with his own thoughts since the accident, and poor Amelia was his only outlet.

"I'm just saying maybe it was for the best, you know? That it happened like this instead of some other way. I mean I wish it hadn't happened at all. Of course, I wish it hadn't happened, but if he had to die maybe it was better that he got to die like this instead of somewhere worse."

Amelia bit back a sob. "What could be worse than this—what the hell are you talking about, James?"

Miller was still in a post-traumatic haze that wouldn't fade for months. "He had to die Amelia. Or it would have kept on happening. He would have kept on going forever. I wasn't going to stop him. You weren't going to stop him. The police didn't even stand a chance."

James was shaking violently as he tried to talk to her, both from his bare suppressed sobs and from the strain that all of this walking and talking was putting on his injuries. Amelia herded him over to some garden furniture in the corner of the garden, out of earshot of the other guests. It did nothing to interrupt his garbled explanations. "He wasn't bad Amelia. You know that he wasn't bad. I'm—I'm not bad, either. I just didn't want him to get in trouble, is all. So I knew about it and I didn't do anything because he is Chris, you know? I'd never do anything that might hurt him."

She took hold of his hands and shushed him. "Calm down. James. Just tell us what happened. What did Chris do?"

He shuddered and then it all spilt out of him like he was regurgitating poison. "He killed them. He just choked the life out of them. I don't know why he did it. I don't even think he knows why he did it. I tried to stop him but he said he'd kill me, too. You didn't know him like I did. You didn't know what he was capable of. What he was really like. I thought he was going to kill you too when I first met you. I was so ha—happy to see you here because it meant that he hadn't gotten to you before the end. You've got to understand. He wasn't a bad guy. You knew him. You know he was a good guy, yeah? It was just he had these black moods and you never knew when they were coming and you never knew what he was going to do when they happened, you know? He could be fine and chatting happily with you one minute and screaming his head off the next. Oh god. He killed a couple of them before I even met him. I don't know what to do about that. I don't know what to do about any of them. Do I tell the police? I mean, what's the point, right? Chris is already—he's done. He's never going to do it again and the girls aren't going to come back just because their families know where they are. What is the point? What's the point of doing anything? Because he's gone now. He's gone..."

James broke down into tears as Amelia stared at him, horrified. When his terrible gulping sobs stopped for a moment she squeezed his hand.

"Chris killed somebody?"

James nodded, hissing as the motion tugged on his injuries. "He killed girls, Amelia. A lot of them. Something was wrong in his brain and it made him go violent and sometimes he would be out on a date and he would just—"

"Shut up, Jim."

He blinked in surprise, tears tumbling from his thick lashes. She leant in closer. "Just keep your mouth shut about all this. All right? There's a lot of folks get killed in the South of Australia without any help from our Chris and I'm not having him made into a scapegoat for every bad thing that's happened here since the bloody British landed. You hear me? Keep your lips together and forget whatever you think you know. Like you said, Chris wasn't like that. He was a good man. One of the last of them. I don't want anybody tainting his memory. Do you hear me?"

James carefully nodded. "I understand."

She took a draw on her bottle of beer and let go of his hand. "Right, bugger off then. We're done."

Distraught and as confused as he had been from the very beginning, James picked himself up and wandered away. Saying nothing to anyone until he was out of the garden, out of the house, and back into the street. Chris had been his whole life. He didn't even know where to go next.

The Investigation

The Australian Police were not familiar with the concept of a serial killer at this point in history. In America, the understanding that would have been required to break this case was being developed in the wake of their own early wave of psychopaths, but in Australia, murders tended to be smaller affairs. There were no needs for grandiose psychological studies to find motives, and there was very rarely a need to look much further than the next-of-kin to find the perpetrator. This is not to say that the police were incompetent, only that they did not have the knowledge required to deal with a crime of this type.

In April of 1978, William Thomas was out searching for mushrooms, just a little off Swamp Road in the barrens, around the township of Truro. It was a pretty common hobby at the time, and he often brought his wife out to enjoy a day in the fresh air and sunshine. You had to be careful, this far out from town, but as long as he planned ahead and brought plenty of water for them both it was safe enough. The animals in the area had a respectable fear of humans, so you didn't have to worry about them too much. There were poisonous snakes and spiders because this was still Australia, but the biggest danger was the heat. For his own protection, William wore a wide-brimmed hat and tried to make sure that he was gone before the midday heat convinced him to take a nap. After an uneventful morning with only a few successes, he came across a long bone poking up from amidst some rocks and assumed that it belonged to a cow. It seemed odd to him that a cow would be out here in the middle of nowhere, but he supposed that stranger things had happened than an animal getting free from one of the ranches and running free. He went on mushrooming with little success until it was almost midday, then he returned home to enjoy the rest of his day off. Something about the bone stuck with him. He mentioned it to his wife, who was just as perplexed as he was, so the next day that the two of them had free, they headed back out to Truro to check it out and continue mushrooming if it turned out that there was no logic to it. It took them a half hour of wandering back and forth before they found the bone again. William was squeamish, so his wife was the one to yank on it. Thanks to a few stray threads of connective tissue, the long bone and some of the others were still connected. When she gave it a tug a shoe popped up. Confused but amused at the odd joke of sticking a woman's jogging shoe onto the end of a cow bone, William pulled the shoe off. Inside they discovered many smaller bones, a patch of skin, and some delicately painted toenails.

The two of them fled back to their car, drove home, and immediately called the police, who arrived shortly afterwards to conduct what they expected to be a routine investigation. The officers found some long-dried blood stains and other bones scattered around. The local scavengers had picked over the poorly buried remains quite thoroughly, going so far as to crack several of the larger bones for marrow. It took crime scene investigators a solid day to piece together enough pieces to confirm that the whole body had been left in this location. Given the location of the body and its current state, it was practically impossible to determine the cause of death, so the coroners had to resort to the time-honored method of making an educated guess. Given the presumed age of the skeleton and the location of the body, it seemed most likely that its previous occupant had decided to go hiking out by Truro without making sufficient preparations. Dehydration had killed more than a few bushwalkers over the years, and given the girl's age, it seemed likely that she would not have had the experience to realise that a quick walk about town in the sunshine was not the same as the punishing heat of the desert-like conditions in the Australian outback. In all likelihood, the hiker had passed out due to the heat and dehydration and never woken up again. Eventually, using dental records and a few key pieces of jewellery around the scene, the body was identified as belonging to the eighteen-year-old Veronica Knight, who had now been missing for over two years, having vanished one night when she was out doing her last-minute Christmas shopping. It seemed unlikely that the girl would travel from the centre of the city out into the middle of nowhere, but there was just no evidence to support any other theory. Teenaged girls did run away from home on occasion, and teenagers, in general, were not above making strange and terrible decisions when given the right circumstances. The case was filed away and forgotten.

Nobody thought anything more of the tragedy until the following year when two hikers came across a second skeleton less than a mile away. Once again, the local wildlife had set upon the body, and it took the police several days of combing the surrounding area to scrape together enough information to make a positive identification of the body as belonging to sixteen-year-old Sylvia Pitman.

Once again, time and animal interference had destroyed most of the evidence, but at least one person in the police department thought that the coincidence of these two young girls being found dead in the same barren stretch of land had significance. Major Crimes Detective-Sergeant Bob "Hugger" Giles had been trying to put together a pattern over the last few months. He had backtracked through all of the missing person's cases in the last few years and found a block of about twelve that remained open, with no new information ever presenting itself. He had been trying to match the missing women to some bodies that had been discovered: a woman who had been shot in the head and buried at a local dump and a second woman, who had been strangled in an apparently unrelated crime of passion. While his attempts to find a connection between the missing women failed, he was still convinced that at least some of the missing women were due to a single murderer.

He pressed forward with an investigation into the bodies as though murders had been committed, starting to assemble a timeline of the deaths and trying to insert his missing women into that timeline. He could not secure the resources from his superior officers to conduct a more widespread search of Truro, so he broke ranks and leaked information about his investigation to the local press. While the Adelaide Police Department may not have wanted to invest time and resources into the killings, the newspapers were willing to offer a hefty $10,000 reward for any information that led to the capture of the presumed murderer. In response to mounting public pressure, the police commissioner announced that the bodies at Truro had "always been considered suspicious" and "had always been investigated as murders" despite all the evidence to the contrary. A taskforce was pulled together from the Major Crimes Unit, but Bob Giles was cut out of the investigation as punishment for speaking to the press. His work was passed off to other officers, who would then go on to lead the hunt for the Truro Killer. A search was conducted in the area where the first two bodies were found and turned up nothing, but when it was extended to include the empty paddocks on the opposite side of Swamp Road, they quickly uncovered a pair of new skeletons. Any hopes of a coincidence were abandoned and the full weight of the police department was thrown into the investigation. The two bodies were eventually matched up to a pair of missing girls from Giles' timeline: Connie Lordanides and Vicki Howell.

With the discovery of the new bodies, the public uproar grew, as did the pressure on the local government in Adelaide to resolve the situation as quickly and quietly as possible. The $10,000 reward that had been placed in the local newspapers was replaced with a more substantial $30,000 by the local aldermen. Historically, serial killers have not been caught by this kind of public appeal because the only people with knowledge of their crimes are the perpetrators and victims. The isolation and compartmentalization that allow serial killers to operate without detection also protects them from the usual methods that the police use to catch garden variety murderers. While your average murderer succumbs to guilt or pride and lets details of their crime slip, a psychopath literally does not care about the opinions of other people so feels no compunction to discuss their crimes either way. Usually, a criminal conspiracy is broken by finding one of the members who are willing to turn in the others in exchange for leniency or reward. Leverage is the key, but with serial killers, there is no psychological weak point to apply pressure to.

If it hadn't been for the increased reward money, then it is more than likely that the truth behind the four known murders and the five others would have gone unknown for the rest of time. But after a year, Amelia's loyalty to her short-term boyfriend Chris had faded in comparison to her loyalty to Amelia. $30,000 now is a substantial amount of money; back in the 70s, it was a life-changing sum, enough to have turned the head of even a well-off woman, and Amelia wasn't even that. The only reason that she had not been down to the police station to claim the original $10,000 reward was that she had not made the connection between Miller's rambling story at the funeral and the murders that were being reported on the news. It was only when a map of the dumping grounds was published that she realised that it referred to the area where Chris used to like to take her for a quiet night out.

From there, tracking down James Miller became the police's sole avenue of inquiry. There was nothing in the story that Amelia told that could not have been fabricated, and indeed she had certainly embellished parts of it with details about murders committed with guitar strings and other fanciful notions, but the key facts that she was able to deliver told them some very important things. She was able to tell them the date that Chris had been released from prison, which was a short time before the first girl on their timeline went missing, and she was able to tell them when Worrell died, just eight days after the final victim vanished. The timeline lent far more credence to her stories than the shaky details that she used to fill in the gaps. The new lead on the case was Detective Sergeant Glen Lawrie, and while he didn't like the politics behind the move that had put him in charge, he was still more than ready to dive into the work. He had picked up Giles' plans seamlessly and continued to use his list of missing girls and his proposed timeline as the bible from which the case was run.

Miller proved trickier to find than might have been anticipated. He had lost his job almost immediately following Worrell's death. His workmates and his boss had plenty of sympathy for him and had treated the man as though he had lost a spouse rather than a friend due to their close relationship, but even if Miller had chosen to show up to work when he had agreed to, the injuries that he had sustained in the car crash made it unlikely that he would have been able to continue doing the gruelling manual labour of a roadwork crew, anyway. He spent all of his time in the apartment that he used to share with Chris, sorting through the other man's sparse belongings and reliving old memories. It wasn't long before his sister approached him, against the wishes of her husband, and invited James to come and live with them again until he could get his life back in order. He refused to be separated from the few things that he had left to remind him of his beloved. The next time that she tried to get in touch, she discovered that his phone had been cut off. It wasn't long after that his landlord evicted him from the apartment for failing to pay rent. The few belongings that he was able to save went into the Valiant. The rest were sold off by the landlord to try to recoup his losses.

What happened to him after that eviction is a little hazy. He lived mostly in the car that had been his and Chris' special place, although on occasion he spent time in a few of the homeless shelters around Adelaide. Normally, this would have been the point at which Miller got back on the road to go looking for new itinerant work, but he seemed to have lost all of his passion and drive. The police discovered that he was definitely still hanging around Adelaide on the first year's anniversary of Worrell's death because he had placed a memorial in the local paper. A poem in commemoration of his friend.

"Worrell, Christopher Robin.

Memories of a very close

friend who died 12 months

ago this week, Your friendship

and thoughtfulness and kindness,

Chris, will always be

remembered by me, mate.

What comes after death I can

Hope, as I pray we meet again"

After realising that he had been homeless for most of the time since the death of Worrell, the police began contacting the local charities and shelters to try and find someone matching his description. Before long, they were put in touch with the new Adelaide's Central Mission, where Miller was currently doing odd-jobs and running errands in exchange for his room and board. The Central Mission must have loomed large in Miller's consciousness, another huge religious-run establishment, like the reformatory that he had first been condemned to as a child, but he worked for them without complaint, finding some sort of comfort in his destitution. Detective Sergeant Lawrie assigned eight plainclothes detectives to watch Miller at all times to make sure that he did not slip through their fingers. The hope was that by following him they might be able to gather more information beyond hearsay and conjecture that they would be able to use to press forward with a conviction. It lasted for less than a day before Miller spotted them. He wasn't a master criminal by any means, but he was more than capable of picking out a policeman, no matter what they were wearing. The chase that followed was brief and almost comically pathetic. Miller was malnourished, his body had never fully recovered from the car accident that destroyed his life, and the police were all at least a decade younger than him. He was taken into custody within moments of trying to run, and he admitted that he had been following the case in the papers and was expecting to see them sooner or later.

In an interrogation room, Detective Sergeant Lawrie sat with Miller and began to present their evidence. He laid out the details that they had already collected, but Miller denied everything. He didn't know anyone called Chris. He didn't know any Amelia. He didn't know any of these girls. When Lawrie presented him with the signed statement from Amelia, he admitted to knowing her and remembering her boyfriend, but denied everything beyond that. They pressed him for details about certain girls, certain dates, and he told them that he didn't remember a thing. James Miller had never been any good at standing up against the police when his own neck was on the line, but now that he was defending the memory of his lover, he was stalwart in his cries of ignorance. Lawrie laid out pictures of the girls on the table in front of him. He forced him to look into the faces of the innocent girls that Chris's unholy lust had led him to kill. James denied and denied and denied. Lawrie thought that he had the measure of Miller, a feeble and effeminate character who would not hold up under any serious pressure. He did not know that pressure was what had shaped Miller into the man he was today, brittle and bitter when confronted with force but incredibly weak in the face of the slightest kindness. After six hours of relentless questioning, Lawrie was ready to admit defeat and cut Miller loose until they could find some sort of evidence to use to pressure him into talking later. He got up to leave and casually offered Miller a coffee. The complete breakdown into sobbing that came afterwards was as much of a shock to the police as it seemed to be to Miller. When he had finally stopped crying and been given his coffee, he said, "Amelia's only doing what I should have done from the start. I should have told you right from the start, but you've got to know I didn't do anything wrong. I just drove the car. I just—I just cared about Chris, you know? I just wanted him to be happy."

Lawrie was about to leap in when Miller asked for a few minutes to "get his thoughts lined up."

When the police returned to the room, Miller said, "If I can clear this up, will everyone else be left out of it? I suppose I've got nothing else to look forward to whatever way it goes. I guess I'm the one who got mixed up in all of this. Where do you want me to start? I drove around with Chris and we picked up girls around the city. Chris would talk to the girls and get them into the car and we would take them for a drive and take them to Truro and Chris would rape them and kill them. But you've got to believe that I had nothing to do with the actual killings of those girls."

Lawrie played up his sympathy for the man, patting him on the back. "We understand that you loved Chris and you just wanted to protect him. That is what everyone is going to know."

The idea of his love for Chris finally being public knowledge rather than a dirty little secret seemed to give James the strength that he needed to press on. He looked up at the Lawrie and said, "There's three more of them. I can show you where to find them."

Even though it was ten o'clock at night, after the intense six-hour bout of questioning, the police took him out to find the graves. Along with Lawrie was a heavily armed escort to ensure that there was no possibility of Miller escaping. They were under a lot of pressure to solve this case, and they didn't want their perfect solution getting a scare and heading for the hills. Out at Truro, Miller walked side-by-side with Lawrie, leading him through the pitch black to a spot by a hillside where a tree had toppled onto its side to shelter the shadowy patch of earth beneath. Lawrie turned on his flashlight, and the grinning skull of Juliet Mykyta stared out of the shadows at him. Later, Lawrie would say that this was the moment that he became certain Miller had lied to them about his involvement in the killings. "He had told us in the interview a few hours earlier that he walked into the bush while his male partner killed the girls. He said he was only the driver. But it was just inconceivable that he could find this spot off a dirt track, in the dark, and then walk us straight to her if he was not directly involved."

At Wingfield, James had no problem pointing out the two graves. When asked the names of the victims he denied knowing them. "Chris did all the talking. I just tried not to think about it."

When they arrived at Port Gawler, he had a harder time finding the gravesite because Chris had dug it himself and one patch of sand looked much like another. Eventually, he found the spot and the crime scene investigators began their careful excavations. By the end of the night, all three of the new bodies had been recovered and linked to the respective missing person's files. As the sun rose, James Miller was charged with seven counts of murder.

Trial and Punishment

Miller's trial finally took place in 1980. He pleaded not guilty to all seven charges of murder. His defence laid out a story in which Miller was a terrorised victim of Worrell, just as the girls had been, cowed by the younger man's brutality but, even so, unwilling to commit any crime for him beyond driving him around town as he went to collect his victims. He claimed to have resisted Chris to the very end. To have been horrified by the things that the man did but too entrapped by the time that he realised what was going on to come forward. He acted like he was the betrayed party in his interactions with the police. After gifting them with all of the information he had on the murders, he was shocked to be accused of committing them. His closing statement was that he would gladly admit to guilt in not informing the police about Worrell's crimes and serve out the rest of his days in prison for it, but he would not accept responsibility for Chris's crimes on top of his own. He was, by this point, so obviously heartbroken at the loss of his lover that the jury was beginning to show sympathy for him. Sympathy that he quickly lost when the defence asked if he would ever have turned Chris in. He answered truthfully before his lawyer could stop him. "If Chris was still alive and he was still out killing girls every night, I would still be out there driving him and not saying a word. I would never betray Chris."

The prosecution painted a very different picture of events, framing Miller as an active participant in the murders. His stories of Chris's overwhelming charm did not seem to measure up to reality. No young girl would willingly get into the car with two strange men, according to the prosecutor. Miller must have been present to help Chris manhandle his victims into the car, and he likely drew sexual satisfaction from indulging his lover's hedonistic desires despite the terrible damage that they did. There was a fierce exchange with the defence, who claimed, somewhat correctly, that Miller was being used as a scapegoat for the state to assign all of the blame for crimes for which the true perpetrator was now beyond the court's reach to punish. The prosecution replied that Miller was trying to sell the jury a fantasy in which murder victims frolic gaily to their deaths without any attempts at a struggle. If no violence was used, then the crimes would have been impossible, so at least some part of Miller's version of events was deceitful.

Details of the crimes that Miller had not previously been aware of were revealed during the trial, shocking and appalling him just as much as the jury. He did not know the level of violence that Chris had inflicted on some of his later victims, believing that only the strangulation had taken place. He did not know that Chris had used a wire to choke one of the girls, that he had beaten another as he raped her or that one of the girls had been buried alive with sand found in her airways when the corpse was recovered. He had no idea about any of these details, and he made that clear to the court, but it didn't matter. It was like a man saying that he did not know how much damage a bullet was going to do after he had already pulled the trigger. Whatever his intentions had been, they mattered much less than the results, and the results were seven dead girls who had been raped, tortured, and disposed of with less respect than many people grant to their rubbish.

The jury's deliberations were relatively short for such a massive trial. Less than an hour later, James Miller was convicted of six of the killings, every one of them except the first, giving him the benefit of the doubt that he genuinely did not know what his best friend had intended up until the moment that he returned to the car and saw the body. Justice Matheson sentenced Miller to the maximum that he could, six consecutive life sentences.

As he was dragged out of the courtroom to face his fate, he screamed, "You're a liar Laurie. You're a damned liar. You know I didn't do anything. You know I never touched them. You're sending me down for nothing. I never even touched them!"

Laurie's testimony about the state of the bodies and what the police had been able to extrapolate from the information that they had gathered had been a major contributor to the narrative that the prosecution had been trying to create. Miller did not seem to understand that the sympathy the detectives had shown towards him had been manipulation. Miller and his criminal companions may have been accomplished liars, but they were amateurs compared to the police. James might have lied to separate people from their valuables, and Chris might have lied to separate them from their lives, but men like Detective Sergeant Laurie lied to separate the wolves from the flock. It was their stock and trade, and while Miller was never the greatest mind in the room, Laurie had outplayed him so thoroughly that even now he couldn't understand it.

In the years that followed, there would be considerable legal battles fought over Miller's status as a murderer, and the case would help to shape precedent for the whole Australian justice system. He was convicted of the murders on the basis that he was part of a joint criminal enterprise, a law that was more commonly used to punish members of the organised crime syndicates that had begun to infiltrate the larger cities. The argument was that he was present at each of the crime scenes and that, through his actions, he made the crimes happen, even if he was not involved in the specific acts themselves.

Years later, one of the jurors in his original trial petitioned the secretary general for a retrial after realising that he and his fellow jurors had been ordered by Justice Matheson to find Miller guilty before their deliberations. Despite this being recorded in the court stenographer's reports, the attorney general refused to grant a second trial. The appeals process in Australia is nothing like the one in America or the United Kingdom, so a retrial was genuinely the best option for Miller to see what he considered to be justice. He campaigned for retrial constantly throughout his years in prison, making use of his notoriety in the years that followed to have memoirs published that he hoped would exonerate him—memoirs upon which most of the writing about the Truro Murders has actually been based, resulting in a massive bias in modern reporting in his favour. Of course, he was the only participant in the events who was still alive to tell his tale, so it is no surprise that the many people through the years who were fascinated by the bizarre tandem killers heard his version of events.

Four years into his sentence, while still campaigning for a retrial, Miller undertook a hunger strike to highlight the injustice that had been done to him. The strike lasted for forty days and was bringing him a lot of attention in the press and public consciousness. People had forgotten the terror that they felt during the killing spree and the consequent discovery of the bodies, and without that emotional backbone, it was easy to see that Miller may very well have been used as a scapegoat to ease the public's worry about killers roaming free. He quickly lost public support after choosing to stand behind the deceased Worrell at his own expense. In a televised interview he declared, "Chris Worrell was my best friend in the world. If he had lived, maybe 70 would have been killed. And I wouldn't have ever dobbed him in."

The prospect of so massive a spree seems to be supported by criminological studies into the behaviour of serial killers. Chris was escalating the pace and viciousness of his attacks in a manner that was consistent with what is known of sadistic sexually motivated serial murderers. He would have gone on killing more and more viciously and rapidly until he was taking multiple victims in a single day. It is usually only at the peak of their escalation that a serial killer would manage to kill four victims in a single week, so it is terrifying to imagine what heights Worrell might have reached. The usual end to this pattern of escalation is a berserk period where the killer is exposed to the public eye, but thanks to the way that Worrell committed his crimes, it is just as possible that he would simply have continued abducting women off the street until he was eventually captured by luck. It took two years for the police to even acknowledge the possibility of a serial killer, despite all of the women who had gone missing. How many more would have died in those two years? Even if Worrell had gone against the trend and slowed down instead of escalating further, the body count would still have been catastrophic.

Regardless, James never received his retrial. He remained in the very same prison where he had served out his two sentences with Chris, Yatala. He walked the same yard where he had first met his lover's eyes. He slept in a cell the very same as the one where he had first laid down and dreamed of Chris. Everywhere that he went, he was followed by the ghost of Chris Worrell. Every moment was filled with bittersweet memories of the one he loved.

The campaign for a retrial ground to a halt as the public forgot all about him. His hopes of being vindicated of a crime that was now part of the country's legal library grew slimmer by the day, and they weren't too broad to start with. When he gave up on his attempts to have his jail sentence revoked, he was able to turn his attention in a more productive direction. He may have claimed that he had nothing to live for when he was arrested, but it seemed to be a lot easier to have nothing to live for in the comfort of your own home rather than a prison cell. After years of pointless legal battles, the few lawyers who were still willing to work with Miller were relieved to be given a new avenue to pursue. He began to petition the courts to set a date for him to seek parole. There was still a small but vocal contingent of the Adelaide community who considered Miller to be the psychopathic monster that his lover was. In death, Chris had left a permanent mark on James, as surely as if he had declared their relationship from the rooftops. It seemed to give James some satisfaction to know that his name and Chris's would be tied together forever in history. Their names forever married on crime reports and urban legends. The vocal contingent opposed to his release had been asleep on the job over the last few decades while James ran a steady but quiet PR campaign from within his cell. He appeared in front of the justices as a harmless old man, and he had been playing up his innocence for decades. They granted him the earliest parole date that the law would allow: the year 2014.

Unfortunately for James, his life had not been the easiest one, and it was all beginning to catch up with him. During a routine check-up in the prison hospital, it was discovered that he had been living with Hepatitis C for most of his adult life. He began treatment to deal with the symptoms and returned to his cell with no awareness of the significance of the illness or the seriousness. He had always felt terrible, so the knowledge that some part of that came from a sickness rather than him wasn't really cause for alarm. In another regular check-up in the early 2000s, the doctor discovered that his prostate was enlarged and ordered a biopsy. When the results came back, James had to add cancer to the long list of things that were making his life terrible. While they aggressively treated the cancer to the best of their ability, and they genuinely believed that it had been destroyed, it was not long before he began showing symptoms again. When it returned, the cancer took not only his prostate but also spread to his lungs. Soon, he was too weak to leave his cell—although the prison hadn't been asking the now elderly Miller to do hard labour in a very long time. In 2008, he was transferred to the Mary Hope Hospice Center to live out his final days in relative comfort, and late one October night he passed away in his sleep, still six years away from parole. He had survived long enough to become the longest serving prisoner in the whole of Southern Australia, just not quite long enough to be released. The autopsy confirmed that his death was due to liver failure as a complication of his Hepatitis, but by that point, it was really only a matter of time before one or another of his various health problems finished him off. There was no doubt that he had received the very best of care, even if many would argue that he did not deserve it.

Very few people received a call to inform them of his death. The warden of Yatala was one. His niece was another. The only one who spoke about his death publicly was Niki Lamb, the daughter of Deborah Lamb, the duo's final victim. Niki had consistently blamed Miller for the murder of her mother, regardless of whatever extenuating circumstances he tried to use as an excuse. She said, "His death is a massive relief. There will never be an end to the evil that he did because I will never have my mother back, but it is the end of a dark chapter and the beginning of a new one."

Even on his deathbed, James offered no words of apology or admission to his crimes. He insisted until the very end that Chris was solely responsible for the killings, although later interviews with inmates at Yatala indicate that this was not the case. In conversation with the few prisoners who had taken the time to get close to him, Miller had admitted that he had a sort of pact with Chris, an agreement that they wouldn't let a single witness to their crimes live. A deal that there would be no survivors to identify them. It sounded like the sort of promise that a psychopath might make to his faltering accomplice when he was scared of being caught, and it cast doubt over the truth of all Miller's claims of innocence through the years.

For James, death was probably the greatest gift he could have received. In life, he had no hope at happiness. He was condemned to spend the rest of his days as one of the most loathed criminals in Australian history, trapped in a prison without friends, family, or hope. More importantly, he was separated from the love of his life. In death, the agnostic Miller might have at least hoped that he would have a chance to see his beloved Chris Worrell again. If it hadn't have been for his lifelong cowardice, James probably would have taken that path to freedom a long time ago.

Conclusion

There are very few serial killers who work in tandem, but as a rule among that rare group, there is always one who is dominant and one who is submissive. One who leads and one who follows. We will never know what dark roads Worrell would eventually have led Miller down if he had lived. It is quite possible that he would have had the other man doing his killing for him by the end of it, as often happens. It was very lucky for the people of Adelaide that Worrell's tire happened to blow at the exact moment that it did because it seems like it spared them a season that would have made the Summer of Sam seem like a relaxing vacation by comparison.

The dominant and submissive relationship is profoundly related to the way that serial killers experience the world. They do not have a sense of right and wrong, they do not understand human emotions beyond the surface levels that they emulate to manipulate others, but they do understand that if someone stronger forces them to submit then that is what they must do and that if they find someone weaker than them they can force them into submission themselves. Worrell found himself a willing submissive in Miller, someone who was willing to completely sublimate all of his own needs to see to it that his lover felt fulfilled. Someone who drew pleasure from submitting to his master. If complete power over a single person had been enough for Worrell, then there would be no book in your hands right now. There would just have been a kinky gay couple enjoying an alternative lifestyle in the Adelaide suburbs, probably to this day. But Worrell wanted more than just one person in his power. He wanted everyone. He wanted the thrill of claiming new prey and dominating them. It wasn't the pursuit of sex that drove him to rape, and it wasn't an attempt to cover up those rapes that led to the killing—it was all about power from start to finish. Worrell wanted to prove his power over these girls, and killing them was the ultimate way to stake his claim, to declare to the universe that his pleasure was worth more than their lives.

Christopher Robin Worrell was a monster. There can be no denying the fact that he murdered girls, some as young as 15, just for his own sick satisfaction. He is the perfect fit for the psychological model of a classic sadistic serial killer, from his behaviour to his motivations. If he had worked alone, he would have been almost unremarkable in that particular field and, of course, he would have gotten away with his crimes forever.

The sexual sadist is not inherently evil. Most sadists are perfectly pleasant people who have a sexual interest that is slightly outside of the norm. Many of the people reading this book probably have a streak of it themselves. It is only when sadism combines with a hedonistic pursuit of pleasure at all costs that we enter into dangerous territory. Even then, there are no shortage of hedonistic sadists roaming about the world who somehow do not transform into nightmarish monsters trying to slaughter their way through the local population. Psychopathy is the final ingredient to make this kind of killer—the absence of remorse and the inability to understand that other people are just as real as you are. There is a moment in a child's mental development when they come to understand that the people around them have the same inner life as the child, that they are fully fledged people with the full range of emotions and thoughts, not just marionettes moving through the world. The psychopath never has this development. To them, there is only one person in the entire world: themselves. If there is only one real person in the world, then their happiness becomes the moral imperative. Nothing is wrong as long as it brings them pleasure.

James Miller was not a monster. He was a deeply flawed and confused human being who saw a cunning and vicious predator and mistook it for the love of his life. He had spent a lifetime neglected and shown no affection, in part because of his sexuality but also simply because he was unlucky in the circumstances of his birth. He cuts a fairly tragic figure, and it is no surprise that he found champions who were willing to fight the legal system in an attempt to free him from prison.

None of this is an excuse for his crimes. If anything, it makes him even more guilty than Worrell, because James had a sense of right and wrong. He knew that what he was doing was evil and he just didn't care. He didn't care that his actions led to the death of those seven girls or that they would have led to the deaths of seventy more. He would have done anything for the man that he was smitten with, regardless of how it clashed with his own morals. He made the decision to set those morals aside. He weighed up everything that he knew was right against the chance to win the heart of a dark-eyed boy with a winning smile, and he chose the selfish path.

Love makes fools out of us all.

RYAN GREEN

RYAN GREEN

RYAN GREEN

RYAN GREEN

About the Author

Ryan Green is a true crime author who lives in Herefordshire, England with his wife, three children, and two dogs. Outside of writing and spending time with his family, Ryan enjoys walking, reading and windsurfing.

Ryan is fascinated with History, Psychology and True Crime. In 2015, he finally started researching and writing his own work and at the end of the year, he released his first book on Britain's most notorious serial killer, Harold Shipman.

He has since written several books on lesser-known subjects, and taken the unique approach of writing from the killer's perspective. He narrates some of the most chilling scenes you'll encounter in the True Crime genre.

You can sign up to Ryan's newsletter to receive a free book, updates, and the latest releases at:

WWW.RYANGREENBOOKS.COM

More Books by Ryan Green

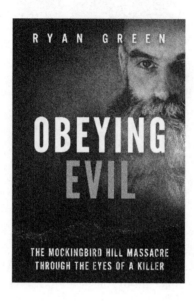

In 1979, Simmons retired as an Air Force Master Sergeant following 20 years of service. The instability that followed his military days exacerbated his desire for control over his family. Simmons used intimidation, humiliation, and violence to assert dominance over all but one of his family members. He allowed a softer side to surface for his favourite daughter, Shelia, whom he forced into an incestuous relationship and eventually fathered her child.

His need for total control led to isolation within his family and an inability to hold down a job. His frustration grew to untold levels when Sheila left the family home and married another man. With his plans in ruin and his grip softening, Simmons surprisingly supported his family's desire for a big Christmas celebration. The stage was set for a heartwarming reunion but he had laid a very different set of plans.

More Books by Ryan Green

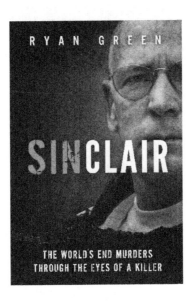

On 15th October 1977, Christine Eadie and Helen Scott left the World's End pub after a fun-filled night with two men in their arms. They had their whole lives ahead of them. They had nothing to fear and everything to look forward to.

Their naked bodies were discovered the following day. They were found six miles apart from each other. No attempt had been made to conceal their bodies, and both girls had been beaten, gagged, tied, raped and strangled.

The case attracted widespread media attention and despite the Police's best efforts, they were unable to identify a culprit. Within the next six months, the investigation was scaled down. The World's End killers were still at large. Free to continue terrorising the streets of Scotland.

More Books by Ryan Green

In the fall of 1994, Erich Baumeister (13), was playing in a wooded area of his family's estate, when he stumbled across a partially buried human skeleton. He presented the disturbing finding to his mother, Julie, who inquired about the skull to her husband, Herb. He told her that the skeleton belonged to his late father, an anaesthesiologist, who used it for his research. He said he didn't know what to do with it, so he buried it in the back garden. Julie believed him.

Over the course of eighteen-months, Julie became increasingly concerned and frightened by her husband's mood swings and erratic behaviour. In June 1996, whilst Herb was on vacation, she granted police full access to her family's eighteen-acre home. Within ten days of the search, investigators uncovered the remains of eleven bodies. Once news of the findings at Fox Hollow Farm was broadcast, Herb disappeared.

Free True Crime Audiobook

Listen to four chilling True Crime stories in one collection. Follow the link below to download a FREE copy of *The Ryan Green True Crime Collection: Vol. 2.*

WWW.RYANGREENBOOKS.COM/FREE-AUDIOBOOK

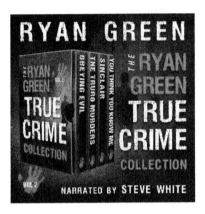

"A very sick set of murders but an excellent account that is impossible to put down." –**Ttneff**

"I found this book to be very well written, but very terrifying! Ryan Green is an incredible storyteller...he doesn't just tell the story, he allows you to be part of it." –**Blackbird**

"Ryan Green ranks at the top of my list for true crime authors. I can't wait for the next book." –**KB Webster**

"Green weaves the tale expertly with just the right amount of detail." – **Kelly Watley**

WWW.RYANGREENBOOKS.COM/FREE-AUDIOBOOK

Printed in Great Britain
by Amazon

83835056R00088